Decision Making in Police Enquiries
and Critical Incidents

Mark Roycroft · Jason Roach
Editors

Decision Making in Police Enquiries and Critical Incidents

What Really Works?

Editors
Mark Roycroft
Open University
Milton Keynes, UK

Jason Roach
Applied Criminology and Policing
Centre
University of Huddersfield
Huddersfield, UK

ISBN 978-1-349-95846-7   ISBN 978-1-349-95847-4   (eBook)
https://doi.org/10.1057/978-1-349-95847-4

Library of Congress Control Number: 2018958599

© The Editor(s) (if applicable) and The Author(s), under exclusive licence to Springer Nature Limited 2019
The author(s) has/have asserted their right(s) to be identified as the author(s) of this work in accordance with the Copyright, Designs and Patents Act 1988.
This work is subject to copyright. All rights are solely and exclusively licensed by the Publisher, whether the whole or part of the material is concerned, specifically the rights of translation, reprinting, reuse of illustrations, recitation, broadcasting, reproduction on microfilms or in any other physical way, and transmission or information storage and retrieval, electronic adaptation, computer software, or by similar or dissimilar methodology now known or hereafter developed.
The use of general descriptive names, registered names, trademarks, service marks, etc. in this publication does not imply, even in the absence of a specific statement, that such names are exempt from the relevant protective laws and regulations and therefore free for general use.
The publisher, the authors and the editors are safe to assume that the advice and information in this book are believed to be true and accurate at the date of publication. Neither the publisher nor the authors or the editors give a warranty, express or implied, with respect to the material contained herein or for any errors or omissions that may have been made. The publisher remains neutral with regard to jurisdictional claims in published maps and institutional affiliations.

Cover illustration: © Melisa Hasan

This Palgrave Pivot imprint is published by the registered company Springer Nature Limited
The registered company address is: The Campus, 4 Crinan Street, London, N1 9XW, United Kingdom

CONTENTS

NOTES ON CONTRIBUTORS

Prof. Robin Bryant is Director of Research and Knowledge exchange within the Department of Law and Criminal Justice at Canterbury Christ Church University. The Department carries out various funded research activities within the criminal justice sector. His research interests include the investigative decision making employed by detectives and he is an external examiner for a number of Universities in the UK on Policing and Criminology programmes. He has published books and journals on investigation and police training. He has published and presented widely on investigative theory.

Read more at https://www.canterbury.ac.uk/social-and-applied-sciences/law-criminal-justice-and-computing/staff/Profile.aspx?staff=bb4c23af295d4844#tGqgyheqm8Ej08KM.99.

Declan Donnelly is a retired Metropolitan Police Service (MPS) detective superintendent. He served 32 years in the MPS, of which 28 were as a detective. In 1998, he was seconded to the National Crime Faculty at the National Police Staff College as part of a small National team to devise and develop the first National SIO development course. He has investigated a wide range of serious crime including homicide investigations as a senior investigating officer. Following the 2001 'world trade centre' terrorist attack as staff officer to the Deputy Assistant Commissioner Security, he helped co-ordinate the MPS response. In 2008, he was seconded to the Royal Cayman Islands Police Service to write and develop their policy in relation to Professional Standards. As a police officer, he has attained an LLB (Hons) and an M.Sc. in Forensic and Legal Psychology. On retirement, he became Director of Regulation for the Greyhound Board of Great Britain and was responsible for reforming the response to regulation and welfare. He is now studying full time at Anglia Ruskin University for a Ph.D. researching the factors influencing decision making by SIOs in cases of stranger homicide.

Ivar Fahsing is a Detective Superintendent of the Norwegian Police Service and an assistant professor at the Norwegian Police University in Oslo. He has served with Oslo Police's murder squad and KRIPOS, the section dealing with national organised and serious crime. He has published books on organised crime and police investigation. He teaches investigative techniques and forensic psychology at the Norwegian Police University. His Ph.D. was entitled the "Expert Detective" and he has researched investigative decision making.

Adam Harland grew up in London, before joining the Metropolitan Police in 1983. Educated at Haberdashers Aske's, Elstree and Downing College, Cambridge, he has a further postgraduate degree in Policing Studies from Exeter University. Subsequently moving to Yorkshire, he has specialised in investigation of fraud, homicide and conduct in public office for more than 20 years. Since retiring as a senior detective he has continued to assist and direct major enquiries and currently heads a joint force 'Cold Case' team. Unsurprisingly, he remains in 'God's Country' with his wife and reportedly grown up children.

Jason Roach is the Director of the Applied Criminology and Policing Centre at the University of Huddersfield, the Editor of the *Police Journal*, and a Chartered Psychologist. Jason has worked in an academic setting for the past 15 years and has previously worked for the UK Home Office and for various Mental Health Services in the North of England. He has published research on a wide-range of topics including; investigative decision making, terrorism, cold-case homicides, and evolutionary psychology and crime, and has also co-authored three books with Prof. Ken Pease, the most recent being *Self-Selection Policing*, in 2016. His main area of research expertise is with police and offender decision making, particularly with regard to the commission and investigation of violent crime, including preventing and investigating child homicide, and the self-selection policing approach to identifying active, serious criminals, from the minor crimes they commit.

Dr. Mark Roycroft is a Senior Lecturer at the Open University and he has lectured on terrorism, organised crime, criminology and investigative theory. He was formerly a Police officer for 30 years in the Metropolitan Police Service with postings in homicide teams, counterterrorism and criminal intelligence. He undertook a Fulbright scholarship to America in 2001 to research major investigations in the United States. His Ph.D. looked at the solving factors in 166 murder cases and the decision making involved by Senior Investigators. He has published a book on *Police Chiefs in the UK* having interviewed 89 Chief Constables, PCCs and heads of Policing agencies. He has written articles on investigative issues, private policing and extremism along with the history of rape investigations.

Adrian West is Adjunct Professor at the Liverpool Centre for Advanced Policing Studies, Liverpool John Moore's University. He is a Forensic Clinical Psychologist who has advised the Police Service on major crime investigations for many years. He has advocated and pressed for more intensive training, examination and qualification for the role of Senior Investigating Officer for a long time.

LIST OF FIGURES

LIST OF TABLES

LIST OF BOXES

CHAPTER 1

Why Understanding Police Investigative Decision Making Is Important

Mark Roycroft

Abstract This chapter sets out the format and content of the book. The author describes Police decision making and evaluates the characteristics of decision making. Police decision making is now more accountable than ever before and current police decision making practice is discussed. The National Decision Model used by the Police is introduced. Police officers of all ranks have to record their decision making and the golden hour tactics are described for those arriving at an incident.

Keywords Police decison making · Evaluating police decision making · Accountability · Solvability factors · Heuristics

M. Roycroft (✉)
Open University, Milton Keynes, UK
e-mail: mark.roycroft@open.ac.uk

© The Author(s) 2019
M. Roycroft and J. Roach (eds.),
Decision Making in Police Enquiries and Critical Incidents,
https://doi.org/10.1057/978-1-349-95847-4_1

1

If you put a step wrong in one of these big cases, you will be guilty for Hell freezing over. (Sarah Payne, mother of murdered schoolgirl Sara Payne, 2006)[1]

Human decision making is a complex phenomenon influenced to varying degrees by a plethora of different variables present at any one given moment. What leads to making a specific decision is often (but not always) influenced, for example, by various contextual, situational, personality, experience and levels of knowledge factors, to name but few. If one considers how evolution has bestowed us humans not simply with brains capable of instant decision making, often referred to as "system one thinking" or "intuition" (e.g. Kahneman 2011) but, should we wish, an ability to engage in more deliberate and thoughtful "system two" decision making (Kahneman 2011), considered "rational thought" by some, for example, whether to follow the satnav directions to the letter, or to ignore its help and follow your own sense of direction and is consistently responsible for the second writer arriving late at most meetings. With all this noise, understanding how decision making occurs is highly complex and far from an exact science and is exemplified no better than when attempting to study decision making in an occupation as complex as policing. The modern police officer, for example, has to contend with a range of concerns before making a decision. The decision making process can be influenced by a unique blend of legal, moral and procedural demands, mixed with community expectations and the reality of the resources available to them. Every police officer has to make a multitude of decisions on a daily basis, some will be minor and routine and relatively inconsequential, but some will be life-changing or life-saving for officer, public or both, irrespective of rank or role. The First officer at a crime scene, for example, must decide how to best preserve evidence which could lead to a conviction, then later may be called to attend a critical incident such as a suspected arson, before helping to defuse a violent situation and all in a day's work. Google "what's an unpredictable job" and police officer will most likely be in the top ten answers offered.

The central question on which this book rests is simply: are police decision makers different from other decision makers in what might be considered to be high risk "critical" (often life or death) situations, for example, hospital doctors, firefighters and soldiers, and if so how do they generally make, and what do they base, investigative decisions in what are termed "critical incidents"? In order to suitably explore this question, we seek to identify what investigative and investigator decision making might be, along with the major internal and external features which influence police investigative decision making in critical incident situations. We seek to shed some light on what Agatha Christie's famous fictional Belgian Detective, Hercule Poirot, refers to as "the little grey cells", but really relates to how police investigators make decisions in critical (in Poirot's sense murder) investigations.

The independent nature of the police officers decision making was highlighted in a 1955 legal case where Viscount Simmons (*Attorney General -v- New South Wales Perpetual Trustees Co [1955] AC 457*) stated that *a constable is an officer whose "authority is original, not delegated, and is exercised at their own discretion by virtue of their office"*.

Arguably, police officers still have a large degree of autonomy in the decisions that they make, for example, whether to give a ticket to someone driving a car with a faulty tail-light or to simply point it out to the driver and accept their promise that they will get it fixed as soon as possible. This is often referred to as "officer discretion", although some would argue that that the abundance of police guidance and procedures in recent years have all but eroded the space for officer discretion, it is a debate for another day and not visited here. We will content ourselves in this book simply to explore wider decision making involved in criminal investigations and other critical incidents.

What factors influence police decision making have long been debated and include environmental factors, legal restraints, organisational factors, politics and situational factors to name but few. Sir Robert Mark, the Metropolitan Police Commissioner opined in his 1978 autobiography that every senior officer has five masters:

1. The criminal law
2. The police authority (now the Police and Crime Commissioners)
3. The staff that they command
4. The public of their district
5. His/her conscience.

Although published in the last century (1978) it can be argued that the five "masters" still stands as an accurate reflection on which the police chief (and any officer) is responsible to.

In more extreme cases, police officers will have little choice but to decide on the "least bad" option in dealing with a critical incident, for example, with a suspected suicide bomber. In the murder case of Becky Godden in Gloucestershire in 2011, for example, the senior detective in charge of the case took the decision to proceed with the suspect (Haliwell) despite not cautioning him first. As a consequence of his actions he then found another victim's body, but at court he was criticised for not giving adequate cautions under the Police and Criminal Evidence Act 1984 to the suspect, Haliwell. Bizarrely, the second murder case was dismissed at court. The Senior Investigating Officer (SIO) in this case decided that the benefits outweighed the disadvantages despite legal guidance. Police decision making relies on professional judgement backed by training and legal constraints.

Retired DCI Steve Driscoll (BBC Stephen Lawrence programme, transmitted 19 April 2018) stated that he "cleared the ground" when he took over the investigation in 2009. This entails thoroughly retracing the steps of the previous investigations and ensuring all avenues of investigation have been exhausted before commencing on new lines of enquiry. The original murder investigation began in April 1993. DCI Driscoll found statements and read through them all and found that the original contact between the suspects and the victim was longer than first thought. He then asked the Forensic Laboratory to reinvestigate certain exhibits and he succeeding in acquiring enough evidence for a retrial of the 2 of the suspects who were found guilty and sentenced in 2012. By "double checking" every available piece of investigation, DCI Driscoll was able to launch a fresh examination of the forensic material which acted as a catalyst to the investigation.

West and Donnelly in Chapter 7 talk of the acquisition of knowledge and good coppering' versus human factors, they too talk of timeliness along with the phases and pressures of homicide investigation today. They talk of "*getting a grip of the investigation*" (pp. 117 and 118 of Chapter 7), a complaint made by the (Flanagan) HMIC report into the running of the investigation into the murder of Holly Wells and Jessica Chapman in Soham in 2002. Stuart Kirby in his book "Effective Policing" (2015) discusses the principle of "clearing the ground beneath your feet "in an investigation (p. 108). This issue arose in both the Soham murders and the hunt for schoolgirl Milly Dowler's murderer, Levi Bellfield, in Surrey. Kirby suggests three main issues raised by both investigations:

1. Management of information
2. Prioritisation of leads
3. "Lack of grip" of the investigation

All arguably illustrate the flawed decision making inherent in the two cases highlighted.

The main purpose of this book is to identify and explore some of the common characteristics of police decision making in major enquires and critical incidents. Lawrence Sherman (1998) notes the importance of "evidence-based policing" by emphasising the fact that there is little empirical evidence to guide most policing practices—at least this was the case back in 1998. Research on the decision making of criminal investigators is however at best "emergent" and at worst neglected, has tended to focus on particular aspects of the investigative process such as "interviewing suspects and witnesses", detective's "intuition" (e.g. Wright 2013) or how different forms of "cognitive bias" including; confirmation bias (e.g. Rossmo 2009; Stelfox and Pease 2005), "framing effects" (e.g. Roach and Pease 2009) and "tunnel vision" (e.g. Rossmo 2009), can have a negative effect on the decision making of investigating officers in homicide investigations. The book's departure is that it seeks to examine the different stages and types of decision making within enquires and police critical incidents and to gently probe the decision making styles of police officers in an overall attempt to shed-light on how decision-processes work in different critical incident contexts, and not just homicide investigations. (including counterterrorism operations).

Like their predecessors, the modern police officer has to comply with legal statute, Human Rights legislation and the media and ponder whether their actions are necessary and proportionate. Criminal investigation continues to evolve through legislation and case law along with procedural developments and scientific and technical developments have increased the range of material that is now available to SIO. Procedural developments have come about through the lessons learned from public enquires, coroners' inquests, trials and internal reviews. All adding to the complexity of police decision making and we haven't even mentioned the advent of the internet and social media yet!

There is of course no known system of decision making which guarantees infallibility—well not in human beings (homo sapiens) anyway. Optimal decision making often necessitates taking risks even when reasoning to the most likely outcome, which Robin Bryant discusses more fully in Chapter 4. To avoid risk does not ensure success. The police investigator is relied upon to exercise judgment and discretion in their decision making, for example, simply shaking the usual sus-pect tree or raiding a housing estate to round up the "usual suspects", without due thought about the possible/probable consequences, could have unwanted repercussions, including re-enforcing local mistrust and dislike of police, estrangement from the local community, and lead to justifiable claims of human rights abuses. This can be assisted by rigorous training and high professional standards supported by accountability mechanisms such as the IPCC and HMIC. The police differ from other professions in that they have little time for deliber-ation in critical incidents. The police face unique decision making environments which encompass rapidly changing conditions. Chaotic conditions can often create difficulty for police officers in prioritis-ing the direction, type, intensity, and pace of the actions they take to effectively control a critical incident or live investigation. Mullins et al. (2008) proposed a preliminary model with the key factors most likely to influence police decision making within murder investigations. This took into consideration the decision environment, the decision maker and the decision bases. In drafting this model the authors were includ-ing the "individual characteristics of the SIO, the type of investiga-tion, the media and the basis of particular decisions (from intuition to evidence)".

We have seen a vast increase in the transparency of police decision making and the need for police officers of all ranks to justify, record and explain their decision making, particularly Senior Investigating Officer's recording of all decisions they make in specific investiga-tion logs. This move has been heavily influenced by legislation, high-profile reviews such as the Macpherson report and the increased remit and reach of organisations such as the IOPC (Independent Office for Police Conduct, formally known as the Independent Police Complaints Commission).[2] The list of accountability bodies also includes the courts, the media and public inquires such as the Hillsborough inquiry. Roycroft's recent book on Chief Constable's (Roycroft 2016) suggests that although it is right and proper that police officers face scrutiny, the level of scrutiny has increased too dramatically over the last decade.

[2] https://www.policeconduct.gov.uk/.

About This Book

In defence of our credentials for producing a book such as this, one of us has had a career full of first-hand experience of making investigative decisions in many different types of critical incidents, whereas the other has only spent approximately half a career's worth of time observing and researching such decision making in serious cases but of course with the added luxury of having no responsibility for getting these decisions correct. The contributors to this book represent a similar mix of police practitioners and seasoned academic researchers, all with shedding light on decision making in criminal investigations and critical incidents in common, but all with different stories and perspectives to share.

This book sets out to develop the understanding of these decision making processes. Separate chapters will look at decision making in cold cases (Chapter 8),

1. Is the thinking and decision making required in all types of homicide investigation exactly the same? Then if not,
2. Do significant differences exist in the investigation of live, historic and 'cold' case homicide investigations, and are these subject to different types and degrees of cognitive bias?

The decision making in managing major enquires (Chapter 3) Cold case enquires (Chapter 8) and homicide investigations (Chapter 5) arc explored. Ivar Fahsing's Chapter 6 on investigative tipping-points of Norwegian detectives provides an international perspective on investigative decision making in homicide investigations.

The common assumption that all investigations require the same thinking, propagated by investigation guides such as the *Murder Investigation Manual*, is challenged by Harland in Chapter 5 who talks of "timeliness" being a key-factor while Roach in Chapter 8, suggests how confirmation bias and framing, can influence the decision making of the cold case investigator. What Stelfox (2009: 64) describes as adopting the correct "investigative mindset" (also adopted by the *ACPO Murder Manual* 2002) is also questioned here and the development of hypotheses in different policing incidents explored in this book.

In Chapter 9, Roycroft and Roach talk of the solvability factors which often lead to the successful resolution of a case. They argue that these are largely dependent on successful decision making by the senior detective especially those who monitor the "phasing "aspect of enquires. The continual review process is one described in later chapters. The essential skill of continuous review, perhaps on an hourly basis in the original sequence of events of a critical incident can determine and shape the investigative process. As seen in the Stephen Lawrence murder cases and in Rotherham (see Jay Report 2017) if and when investigations go awry they can affect that forces reputation for a generation. Indeed, the management of risk was exposed as a key theme in these investigations and subsequent reviews. Part of the police decision maker's role is to recognise the risk and take appropriate action to deal with it (see Foucault and Anscoff, p. 7, re-risk assessment). Roycroft et al. (2007: 148–162) commented after looking at the socio-historic development of major investigations that

> looking across the historical pattern overall, it does seem that at particular historical moments certain high profile major crime investigations come to be seen as problematic in some fashion (i.e. achieve some measure of amplification). Then the conduct of the investigation itself is enquired into, either through a de facto public enquiry, with the result that some reform in policing practices is recommended.

The reputational damage to police forces and the impact on victims and their families following faulty decision making is considerable with the repercussions lasting decades-the tragedy at Hillsborough in the 1980s serves as testament.

This book will explore some of the psychology behind decision making and the attributes of a good decision maker, along with an examination of the decision making process. In Chapter 4, Bryant states that

> Judgment involves reasoning in practical, non-abstract circumstances and gives rise to action and hence in police critical decision-making is of particular importance. However, sound (valid and reliable) reasoning does not necessarily in, and of itself, lead to the 'correct' judgement being made.

Bryant discusses the role of heuristics in decision making and states that they "can (particularly when applied in ecologically sound circumstances which require rapid decision-making) perform as well, and often better than more formal methods". Heuristics can be used to simplify decisions but as Tversky and Kahneman (1974) state they can lead to systematic errors. They talk of a "taxonomy of themes".

The representativeness heuristic and the availability heuristic have been found to be "most commonly observed heuristics within an investigation" (Kirby 2013). Kirby states that the SIO is open to bias including "belief persistence where once a belief or opinion is formed it can be difficult to override". In Chapter 6, Fahsing explores the educational background of police officers and whether it can influence decision making and if

> expertise seems to make us better, it cannot alone be trusted to serve as a complete safeguard against fundamental cognitive Basis limitations. Enduring high performance in complex operations cannot only rest on individual competence alone.

In Chapter 5, Harland takes us through the Major Incident Room (MIR) procedure the operation of the MIR and the roles and technologies that are employed in analysing the product of investigative activity, and identifying fruitful activity from that analysis. Harland discusses the conflicting demands of control and activity. Harland builds on the theme of timeliness and phasing of enquires. The aim of the book is to reach beyond the police manuals to encompass both theory around decision making and best practice from case studies and research.

RECORDING OF DECISIONS

The modern police decision maker now complete "Decision logs" or "Policy logs". The recording of vital decisions and why certain actions were NOT taken as well as why they were. Cook et al. (2013: 45) discuss the option of "doing nothing" or deferring a decision. They state that it must be done for the right reason and must be communicated to all parties internally and externally, the constant evaluation of facts was shown in Roycroft's (2007) research to be one of the main "solving factors" and this process can help overcome biases and adjust early "bad" decisions.

CURRENT POLICE GUIDANCE ON DECISION MAKING

In the UK, the main police manuals for decision making is the Core Investigative Doctrine and the NPCC Murder Manual. These set out advice on dealing with critical incidents. The Core Investigative Doctrine states that it provides national guidance on the key principles of criminal investigation along with promoting good practice amongst practitioners.

The NPCC Murder Manual breaks the investigative process into 5 stages as follows:

- Stage 1: Fast Track Actions
- Stage 2: Theoretical Processes or Investigative Process
- Stage 3: Planned method of investigation
- Stage 4: Suspect Enquires
- Stage 5: Disposal

The NPCC Core Investigative Doctrine describes some of the issues that investigators face including overcoming personal bias (p. 58) and avoiding verification bias, oversimplifying facts, becoming overwhelmed with information and following non-optimal lines of enquiry. The investigative mindset according to the Doctrine involves the following into the five following principles:

- Understanding the source of material
- Planning and preparation
- Examination
- Recording and collation
- Evaluation.

Stelfox (2009: 148) discuses the reactive and proactive responses to crime investigation with the latter being particularly appropriate to organised crime.

The police in the UK uses the Police National Decision model (NDM app College of Policing accessed 9 August 2016). There are Six key elements with the mnemonic CIAPOAR explaining the key elements of the NDM:

Code of Ethics—Principles and standards of professional behaviour
Information—Gather information and intelligence
Assessment—Assess threat and risk and develop a working strategy
Powers and policy—Consider powers and policy
Options—Identify options and contingencies
Action and review—Take action and review what happened

The College of Policing, Police Code of Ethics (see Appendix 1) sets out the policing principles that members of the police service are expected to uphold and the standards of behaviour they are expected to meet. Many forces have their own values statements which are complementary to the Code of Ethics.

Throughout a situation, decision makers should ask themselves:

- Is what I am considering consistent with the Code of Ethics?
- What would the victim or community affected expect of me in this situation?
- What does the police service expect of me in this situation?
- Is this action or decision likely to reflect positively on my professionalism and policing generally?
- Could I explain my action or decision in public?

During the early stages of an incident, the decision maker defines the situation and clarifies matters relating to any initial information and intelligence. They then assess risk and the NDM asks that Decision makers should consider:

- the options that are open
- the immediacy of any threat
- the limits of information to hand
- the amount of time available
- the available resources and support
- their own knowledge, experience and skills
- the impact of potential action on the situation and the public
- What action to take if things do not happen as anticipated?

THE GOLDEN HOUR

Experienced SIOs often use the term the Golden Hour to describe the principle that effective early action can result in securing significant material that would otherwise be lost to the investigation. This refers to the period following a crime where investigators seek to ensure that all relevant evidence is identified and made secure. Everyone arriving at the scene of a murder has their own golden hour. Where the police are informed of an incident shortly after it has occurred, offenders may still be in the area. Locating them can provide forensic opportunities that could otherwise be lost, the testimony of witnesses can also be obtained while the offence is still fresh in their mind, CCTV images and other data can be collected before it is deleted and action can be taken to secure Scenes before they become contaminated. Cook et al. (2013: 40) summarise the Doctrine as follows:

- Assume nothing
- Believe nothing
- Challenge and check everything. They state that nothing should be accepted at face value or taken for granted. Investigators must "seek corroboration, recheck and review and confirm facts". The Practice advice on Core Investigative Doctrine (College of Policing app) states that investigators should constantly search for corroboration".

These manuals set down the ground rules for decision makers and the book is concerned with the processes that police officers use to reach decisions. The authors (Chapters 2, 3, and 9) research found that experienced senior detectives were concerned with "clearing the ground" beneath their feet once they are engaged in policing an incident, i.e. ascertaining all relevant facts before moving on with an investigation. This includes risk assessment. The philosopher Michael Foucalt stated that his job was to "make windows where there once was walls" (Discipline and Punish the Birth of Prison London 1991). Ansoff and Weston (1962) saw strategy as decision making with imperfect information and he divided management decision making into three. These distinguished decisions as either: Strategic, administrative or operational. The modern police decision maker has to take cognisance of all these issues. Stelfox talks of 3 key decision areas

- Is the behaviour a criminal offence?
- Who might be a suspect?
- What further material needs to be gathered?

In today's environment a fourth element could be added, "the political" element or the perception of how that case is being handled is as important as the "mechanical" conduct of the enquiry. The media, the public and local community will (rightly) demand updates on all elements of the investigation and all concerns will have to be allayed.

References

ACPO Murder Manual. (2002). College of Policing.

Ansoff, H. I., & Weston, J. F. (1962). Merger Objectives and Organization Structure. *Quarterly Review of Economics and Business, 2*(3), 49–58.

Cook, et al. (2013). *Blackstone's Crime Investigator's Handbook.* UK: Oxford University Press.

HMIC Effective Poling. (2015). Home Office.

Jay Report. (2017). *Independent Inquiry into Child Sexual Abuse.* London: HMSO.

Kahneman, D. (2011). *Thinking Fast and Slow.* London: Allen Lane.

Kirby, S. (2013). *Effective Policing Implementation in Theory and Practice.* Basingstoke, UK: Palgrave.

Mark, R. (1978). *In the Office of Constable.* London, UK: Collins.

Mullins, S. J., Allison, L., & Crego, J. (2008). *Towards a Taxonomy of Police Decision-Making in Murder Inquiries.* University of Wollangong.

Roach, & Pease. (2009). The Retrospective Detective: Cognitive Bias and the Cold Case Homicide Investigator. *Journal of Homicide and Major Incident Investigation.* UK: Wiley.

Roycroft, M. (2007). What Solves Hard to Solve Murders. *Journal of Homicide and Major Incident Investigation, 3*(1), 93–107.

Roycroft, M. (2016). *Police Chiefs in the UK: Politicians, HR Managers or Cops.* Palgrave.

Roycroft, M., Brown, J., & Innes, M. (2007). Reform by Crisis: The Murder of Stephen Lawrence and a Socio-Historical Analysis of Developments in the Conduct of Major Crime Investigations. In M. Rowe (Ed.), *Policing Beyond MacPherson.* Routledge.

Sherman, L. (1998). *Evidence-Based Policing, Ideas in American Policing Series.* Washington, DC: Police Foundation. www.policefoundation.org.

Stelfox, P. (2009). *Criminal Investigation.* Cullompton: Willan.

Stelfox, P., & Pease, K. (2005). Cognition and Detection: Reluctant Bedfellows? In M. J. Smith & N. Tilley (Eds.), *Crime Science: New Approaches to Preventing and Detecting Crime* (pp. 191–207). Cullompton, Devon: Willan Publishing.

Tversky, A., & Kahneman, D. (1974). Judgement Under Uncertainty, Heuristics and Biases. *Science, 185*(4157), 1124–1131.

Wright, M. (2013). Homicide Detectives'. *Journal of Investigative Psychology and Offender Profiling*, 182–199. Special Issue: Investigative Decision Making.

CHAPTER 2

History of Decision-Making

Mark Roycroft

Abstract The author looks back over 40 years of inquires and reviews of major police investigations such as The Yorkshire Ripper Case. The author identified 7 themes that run through 40 years of historical enquires, which are: Clarity and leadership among senior officers; Skills of SIOs; Systematic failures; Phasing of enquires; The role of the Major Incident Room; Information management; Individual investigative strategy failures. Past inquiries can help inform present or future investigative strategies by providing best practice and highlighting potential pitfalls. The role of the MIR and Holmes since the Yorkshire Ripper case illustrates the progress that has been made although in the case of the Harper, Maxwell and Hogg murders the suspect was not within the system. The issue of leadership among senior management teams and SIOs was discussed in the inquiries researched.

Keywords Clarity and leadership among senior officers · Skills of SIO's · Systematic failures · Phasing of enquires · The role of the major incident room · Information management · Individual investigative strategy failures

M. Roycroft (✉)
Open University, Milton Keynes, UK
e-mail: mark.roycroft@open.ac.uk

© The Author(s) 2019
M. Roycroft and J. Roach (eds.),
Decision Making in Police Enquiries and Critical Incidents,
https://doi.org/10.1057/978-1-349-95847-4_2

15

This chapter explores the themes from over 40 years of reviews and public inquires into major murder enquires. Seven key themes emerge consistently from this overview. The purpose of the Chapter is to high-light the main issues from the investigations researched and the themes that emerged. Jones et al. (2008: 471) argue for the importance of a his-torical context when examining murder investigations.

Looking across the historical pattern of inquiries, it does seem that at particular historical moments certain high profile major crime investi-gations come to be seen as problematic in some fashion. At such times, the conduct of the investigation itself is reviewed, either through a public enquiry, some other framework or internally, with the result that some reform in policing practices is recommended. The introduction of signif-icant reform is not a continuous progression and development; rather it tends to occur in "fits and starts".

The failure to act quickly as in the Soham (the 2002 murder of Holly Wells and Jessica Chapman) case and the continuation of wrong deci-sions in the Lawrence case were real-life illustrations of the need for skilled decision-making by SIO's. Lord MacPherson in his review of the Lawerence case stated that each bad decision in the initial investigation was compounded.

The Damiola Taylor Review (Recommendation 3.2.8) remarked on the need to appoint people with the skills "to do the job". This was echoed in Recommendation 20 of the Flanagan report into the Soham murder where Sir Flanagan commented that the Chief Officer should (Pimlico lecture 12.1.05) "take a view of the skills needed in a major enquiry and what skills the team actually have and that (in the Soham case) senior officers failed to act on valuable evidential leads gathered by officers on the ground". In the Shipman inquiry Dame Smith criti-cised DI Smith (the SIO), while recognising that many of his mistakes were the result of his lack of experience of criminal investigations of a non-routine nature (see page 5 of the report).

In the Climbie inquiry, Lord Laming stated that an investigation should have begun straight away.

The Macpherson inquiry (into the death of Stephen Lawrence) in rec-ommendation 46.9 stated that when the investigation was handed over to Detective Superintendent Weedon "he perpetuated the wrong deci-sions made in the vital early days. He did not exercise his own critical faculties in order to test whether the right decisions had been made. His fundamental misjudgement delayed arrests until 7th May".

The common theme running through the Byford report, the Lawrence case, the Shipman case and the Soham case is one of leadership. Lord Macpherson commented on the "failure of direction by senior officers (in the Lawrence case p. 317)...who seem simply to have accepted that everything was being done satisfactorily by somebody else". There was a "lack of imagination and properly co-ordinated action and planning". "The Yorkshire Ripper case highlights how the direction given by the SIO can influence the rest of the enquiry. Peter Sutcliffe was interviewed by the Police nine times between 1975 and his arrest in January 1981. Interviewing officers were influenced by the credence given to the letters and the tape sent by a hoaxer.

The review into the investigation of the Omagh bomb attack in N. Ireland (the bomb exploded on 15 August 1998) commented (Orde and Rea 2017, p. 67) there was inadequate management support for and control of the role of SIO" and the HMIC found "little evidence of the idealised Investigative Making Process" and (Orde and Rea 2017, p. 69) there was a two week mindset. This was a complicated investigation involving covert policing, intelligence handling and a joint investigation with the Garda Siochana.

The frequency with which official enquires into homicide are commissioned has increased. This phase started with the Macpherson report in 1999 into the murder of Stephen Lawrence and the review of the Damilola Taylor murder in 2002. The following year saw inquiries into the death of Victoria Climbie and Dame Janet Smith's inquiry into the murders committed by Dr. Shipman. In 2004 Sir Ronnie Flanagan of the HMIC published a report into the murders at Soham. There are now historical inquires into child sexual abuse cases in all parts of the UK including the IICSA, The Independent Inquiry into sexual abuse. The IPCC/IOPC now provides independent scrutiny of police investigations and their work on the Hillsborough case was comprehensive. Table 2.1 highlights the critical issues identified from reviews and inquires from 1966 to the present day.

The present researcher documented themes from each report and then compared them across all reports determining the most frequent. Seven repeated themes emerged:

- Clarity and leadership among senior officers;
- Skills of SIO's;
- Systematic failures;

Table 2.1 Table of recommendations and themes identified from inquiries

Case date of murder	Name and date of inquiry or review	Critical issues	Main recommendations	Themes identified
Cannock Chase Murder 1966	No public inquiry	Failed to identify the suspect		Systematic failures
Murder of Maxwell Confait 1972	Confait enquiry by Sir Henry Fisher 1977	Uncorroborated confession evidence from main suspect having mental age of 8	Tape recording of interviews Introduction of appropriate adults safeguards for vulnerable persons	Accountability of the Police Treatment of vulnerable suspects Skills of SIOs
Murder of Sarah Harper, Susan Maxwell & Caroline Hogg murdered between 1983–1986	No public inquiry	Failure to identify suspect	Catchem database introduced	Systematic failures Management of flow of info
Murder of Stephen Lawrence murdered 22 April 1993	Report by Sir William MacPherson February 1999	Failure to arrest suspects Failure to keep victims family informed	FLO's introduced Decision Logs introduced Racial Awareness Training introduced Murder Review Groups introduced.	Systematic failure Skills of SIO
Murder of Victoria Climbie 25 January 2000	Lord Laming's public Inquiry 2001–2003 reported 2003	Crimes involving children should be dealt with promptly and efficiently	Managers from each service should be involved in the investigation Police must take the lead in any joint investigation Supervisory officers Must take an active Role in Investigations	Skills base Phasing Lack of coordination within the command structure

(continued)

Table 2.1 (continued)

Case date of murder	Name and date of inquiry or review	Critical issues	Main recommendations	Themes identified
Damilola Taylor murdered 27 November 2000	Taylor murder investigation Review report of the over-sight panel December 2002	Post-charge strategy Use of mobile phone evidence Management of witnesses	Evidential opportunities presented by new technologies Murder Investigation Manual (MIM) updated on witness inter-view strategy Amendments to the MIM on witness interview strategy; the management of cell confession evidence and the evidential opportunities presented by new technologies	Lack of clarity among senior officers Skills of SIO's Phasing
Dr. Shipman's murders	Dame Janet Smith July 2003 Inquiry into 15 of Dr. Shipman's patients in July 2003 she reported on the police enquiry of 1998	Pattern of deaths not identified	Standard of (behaviour) of CS Sykes and DI Smith fell below the standard expected by the public GMP should assign SIO's with "appropriate experience" Protocol should be established for low volume crimes New medical coroner service to provide specialised advice CPS to provide a solicitor with medico legal-advice	Lack of clarity among senior officers

(continued)

Table 2.1 (continued)

Case date of murder	Name and date of inquiry or review	Critical issues	Main recommendations	Themes identified
Soham August 2002	HMIC report 2004	Suspect arrested but took 10 days Lack of clarity among SMT Misunderstanding of Critical incident	Understanding of critical incident Systematic shortcomings due to amount of information MIR not fully staffed Confusion at Senior Management level "Golden hours allowed to slip by" "Inability to appreciate the value of the information available" Poorly focused investigation	Skills of SIO's Management of information Lack of clarity among senior officers
SCR into Baby P's death	Peter Connelly died in August 2007 at home in Haringey, north London, after months of abuse	It chastised police for not investigating suspicious injuries Various agencies failed to realise that Stephen Barker, the violent boyfriend of Peter's mother Tracey Connelly, was living at the family home and might have been abusing Peter	Agencies acting in isolation from one another without effective coordination Poor gathering, recording and sharing of information Insufficient supervision by senior management Over-dependence on performance data which was not always accurate	
Lady Justice Hallet 7/7 bombings		that 'major incident' training for all frontline staff, especially those working on the underground, is reviewed	There is room for further improvement in the recording of decisions relating to the assessment of targets	

(continued)

Table 2.1 (continued)

Case date of murder	Name and date of inquiry or review	Critical issues	Main recommendations	Themes identified
Rosemary Nelson case N. Ireland Public enquiry from 2005 to 2011 by retired judge Sir Michael Morland, Dame Valerie Strachan, former chairman of the board of Customs and Excise and Sir Anthony Burden, former Chief Constable of South Wales Police	Loyalist paramilitary group, the Red Hand defenders, claimed responsibility for the murder of the civil rights lawyer Rosemary Nelson on 15 March 1999 in Lurgan. There was no finding of direct collusion by the Army, RUC or state forces. There was a corporate failure to take the threats against her seriously enough—essentially saying those threats were not properly investigated. That officers within special branch and at RUC headquarters regarded Mrs. Nelson as an active supporter of the IRA		Murder investigation The murder investigation was exhaustive, energetic and enterprising. It was not perfect in every respect: The MIT should have made more detailed enquiries into Rosemary Nelson's contacts in the last few weeks of her life The MIT should have documented their thinking about hypotheses other than the obvious one, namely that this was a Loyalist terrorist murder. However, in the main, the investigation was carried out to a high standard, the investigation of the murder was carried out with due diligence	

(continued)

Table 2.1 (continued)

Case date of murder	Name and date of inquiry or review	Critical issues	Main recommendations	Themes identified
Jay report into child abuse in Rotherham 2014	The report found evidence of sexual exploitation of at least 1400 children in Rotherham over this period. The majority of the perpetrators were described as "Asian" by victims. Professor Jay found there was a "collective failure" by both the Council and police to stop the abuse	Police were said to have given CSE no priority, regarding many child victims "with contempt" and failing to act on their abuse as a crime	Police have been trained and resourced to deal with CSE, while there was now a central team in children's social care that worked jointly with police on the issue, the report said	
Casey report into Rotherham 2015	Independent inquiry into CSE in Rotherham 2007 to 2013	From what Inspectors saw, South Yorkshire Police: • did not use alternative ways to gather evidence • did not use alternative strategies to protect victims • did not make use of other tools and powers available to them • did not work effectively with either the community safety or licensing arms of the Council to develop strategies for tackling perpetrators		

(continued)

Table 2.1 (continued)

Case date of murder	Name and date of inquiry or review	Critical issues	Main recommendations	Themes identified
IPCC report into Poppi Worthington case in Cumbria	IPCC report	The IPCC found evidence that Poppi's home was not adequately preserved and searched, resulting in a nappy she had been wearing being lost as potential evidence. There was also evidence indicating that key investigative decisions and policies were not documented, leaving junior detectives feeling 'out of the loop' on how the inquiry was progressing It was the investigator's opinion that police did not adequately investigate whether Poppi had been abused		

- Phasing of enquires;
- The role of the Major Incident Room;
- Information management;
- Individual investigative strategy failures.

These will now be explored in some detail.

CLARITY AND LEADERSHIP AMONG SENIOR OFFICERS

Smith and Flanagan (2000) mentioned leadership as one of their 22 skill clusters for reflective SIOs. They state that an SIO (p. 52) has to be seen to "take responsibility for the investigative process, providing direction". The SIO also needs the ability "to bring pertinent information out of the team". The "good leader" also had the ability to facilitate and maintain control and the ability to inspire the team. The Yorkshire Ripper case highlights how the direction given by the SIO can influence the rest of the enquiry. Peter Sutcliffe was interviewed by the Police nine times between 1975 and his arrest in January 1981. Interviewing officers were influenced by the credence given to the letters and the tape sent by a hoaxer. The common theme running through the Byford report, the Lawrence case, the Shipman case and the Soham case is one of the competences of the SIO. The principle of leadership exposed a lack of clarity which obstructed stages of the investigations. Leadership is a key skill for SIOs and is crucial to the success of the investigation and appeared problematic in the inquires examined. In both the Taylor case and the Yorkshire Ripper case the lack of a clear leader compromised the effective deploying of resources. One person cannot solve the case by themselves and it is the responsibility of all those who assume even partial leadership in key areas.

The Damilola Taylor review (December 2002) commented that the primary investigation was well resourced:

> However, the structure of the oversight and support arrangements and the direct involvement of very senior staff with different roles and responsibilities did lead to a lack of clarity on occasions about where ultimate responsibility for the case as a whole lay.

The review (recommendation 3.3.14) felt that the comprehensive nature of these arrangements and the involvement of so many senior officers may have created a false sense of reassurance about the progress of the investigation. This became *"unhelpful when new problems were encountered in the secondary investigation after the suspects had been sent for trial"*. In recommendation 3.3.16 the panel considered that the MPS should be commended for the scope and scale of Chief Officer Involvement however they commented:

> Certain lines of enquiry were implemented but not adequately resourced (i.e. cell confession evidence). It lacked overall direction and control. The analytical work that was commissioned at an early stage in the enquiry could have been dealt with in a more timely and effective way.

The panel recommended (recommendation 17) that the use of Gold, Silver and Bronze command structures along with other support groups in difficult cases be continued but their nomenclature, purpose and accountability should be "clear." The extent to which these types of command structure can be applied to homicide investigations needs to be clarified. It was further recommended that ACPO identify options and disseminate clear guidance on this issue. The lack of clarity resulting in blurred lines of responsibility can be one of the unintended consequences in critical incidents. This can lead to blurred lines of responsibility and can overcomplicate the line of command. In the Shipman case, the normal police command structure caused confusion. There was a lack of clarity within the command structure and people with the right skills were not placed in the correct positions. In the Shipman Inquiry Dame Janet Smith commented that the primary reason the investigation failed was that:

> Chief Superintendent Sykes instructed DI Smith to undertake the investigation and kept to himself the responsibility for supervision. He was culpably wrong in both respects.

Dame Janet Smith goes on to criticise CS Sykes in other respects and states that he should have realised that DI Smith was out of his depth and it should not have been DI Smith's decision to decide when the investigation was to be closed. Dame Janet also criticises DI Smith, while she recognises that many of his mistakes were the result of his lack of experience of criminal investigations of a non-routine nature. In the report on the Yorkshire Ripper case, Byford (Home Office 1981) commented they were firmly of the view that in cross border series there needs to be one officer in overall command of the investigation with authority to direct the course of the investigation in all the police areas directed.

In the Soham case there was confusion in the first part of the enquiry around the definition of critical incidents. Sir Ronnie Flanagan (HMIC) felt there could have been a

> greater sense of urgency and that the good momentum achieved by the initial officer could have been consolidated.

The report also comments on the difficulties involved in running a "twin track investigation" where the SIO is considering the possibility of both abduction and a murder. This was commented on in the review of the Milly Dowler case Smith (Kirby 2013: 107) and Flanagan (2000) mentioned leadership as one of their 22 skill clusters for SIOs. They state that an SIO has to be seen to take "responsibility for the investigative process, providing direction" (p. 52). The SIO also needs to have the ability "to bring pertinent information out of the team". The Yorkshire Ripper case highlights how the direction given by the SIO can influence the rest of the enquiry. Peter Sutcliffe was interviewed by the Police nine times between 1975 and his arrest in January 1981. Interviewing officers were influenced by the credence given to the letters and the tape sent by a hoaxer.

Skills of SIOs

The skill base of the SIO features in all the inquiries and reviews. Figure 2.1 shows some of the key skills mentioned in the various enquires.

The NPCC (2005) Practice advice Core Investigative Doctrine states that flawed decision-making has been responsible for failed investigations (p. 58). This was echoed by Irving and Dunningham (1993) that the most common factor in the failure of investigations is "flawed decision making". The doctrine further mentions "verification bias" where the detective allows their early assumptions in a case to determine their investigative strategy. Jones et al. (2008) describe this as being where the investigator adopts a hypothesis as to what has happened and then finds the evidence to support his/her hypothesis and excludes contradictory

Skills of SIO	Relevant enquiry
1. Effective Decision Making. The SIO should "Exercise critical faculties"	MacPherson inquiry
2. Planning the Phasing of enquires	Climbie /Taylor review/Byford report
3. Scene Management /Understanding "critical incident" management	HMIC Soham report
4. Witness management	Macpherson report/Soham
5. Strategic investigative awareness/ability to manage investigation	MacPherson inquiry HMIC Soham SCR into Baby P investigation
6. Experience of major investigations	Shipman enquiry/Taylor review
7. Management of the MIR	Macpherson, Rosemary Nelson case
8. Leadership	Byford/MacPherson/ Soham review

Fig. 2.1 Skills of the SIO

evidence. This was very evident in the persistence of the Ripper investigators to build their enquiry around the tape of "Wearside Jack" which later was established to be a hoax. The Damiola Taylor Review (Recommendation 3.2.8) remarked on the need to appoint people with the skills "to do the job". This was echoed in Recommendation 20 of the Flanagan report into the Soham murders. Similarly The IPCC report into Poppi Worthington's death described investigative leads that had been missed and overlooked (see Fig. 2.1). Furthermore junior officers felt out of the loop and this echoes Harland's and Roycroft's finding that the management of the investigation is an important aide to effective decision-making.

Adhami and Browne (1996) suggested that detectives lack inferential judgment and are prone to making fundamental biases and errors of judgment. The failure to act quickly as in the Soham case and the continuation of wrong decisions in the Lawrence case were real-life illustrations of the need for skilled decision-making by SIOs. Lord MacPherson stated that each bad decision was compounded. The selection of lines of enquiry and the current prioritisation and allocation of resources to support them is a key feature of a successful and cost-effective investigation. The inquiries and reviews accentuate the need for careful phasing of the SIOs strategies and actions. The following examples show the need for planning:

- Recommendation 92 of the Climbie inquiry states that crimes involving children should be dealt with promptly and efficiently.
- Recommendation 3.3.16 of the Taylor Review stated that the enquiry lacked overall direction and control. The analytical work that was commissioned at an early stage in the enquiry could have been done in a more timely and effective way.
- In the Yorkshire Ripper case a major error was the excessive credence given to letters and the tapes from John Humble and therefore Peter Sutcliffe should have been arrested earlier.
- Recommendation 3.3.16 of the (Damilola) Taylor Review stated that the enquiry lacked overall direction and control. The analytical work that was commissioned at an early stage in the enquiry could have been done in a more timely and effective way.
- Post-Charge management Recommendation 4.5.3 of the Taylor review states that a number of lines were incomplete at the time the defendants were charged. These included the examination of 86 shoes and trainers seized from suspects and the analysis of mobile telephones.

The Morland inquiry into Rosemary Nelson's murder (2011) said more attention should have been paid to her contacts in the final weeks of her life.

SYSTEMATIC FAILURE

Public enquires into high profile cases such as Stephen Lawrence and Damilola Taylor case have exposed failures in police systems and in policy. The Home Office report 25/04 (Nicol et al. 2004) on reviewing murder investigations noted that many of the serious failures that occur in modern-day complex enquires "*need to be analysed and understood at a systematic rather than individual level*" (p. 13). The report suggests that the organisational culture of the police produces a situation where "provided the investigation gets a result any problems, errors and mistakes can be glossed over" (p. 15). The structuring of the organisational systems and processes can improve the reliability of the investigative process. In the majority of cases researched, there were shortcomings in the resourcing and cross-checking capability of the Major Incident Room (MIR) (see Harland's Chapter 5). This applies to both pre- and post-HOLMES incident rooms. In the Cannock Chase murders of 1966 the police did not identify the murderer in four years. There was no coordination between MIR's as they were in two force areas and pre-Holmes there was no obvious method of sharing information.

Phasing of Enquiries

The planning and phasing of major enquires were referred to in the Climbie inquiry (2003), Lord Laming stated that an investigation should have begun straight away and identified investigative leads that Lord Laming identifies the following as investigative leads that should have been followed:

- The scene of the crime should have been identified
- Statements should have been arranged and obtained from all medical staff
- A full forensic medical examination should have been carried out.
- The likely suspects should have been identified
- Arrangements should have been made to speak immediately to Victoria, independently of any of the suspects, to allow her to speak freely about what had happened to her.

The Macpherson inquiry (into the death of Stephen Lawrence) in recommendation 46.9 stated that when the investigation was handed over to a new SIO:

> he perpetuated the wrong decisions made in the vital early days. He did not exercise his own critical faculties in order to test whether the right decisions had been made. His fundamental misjudgement delayed arrests until 7th May.

In recommendation 46.11 the report comments that the Detective Chief Superintendent allowed himself to go along with the weak and unenterprising decisions made by his SIO's in which he had been himself directly involved. The report criticises the failure to arrest one of the main suspects, Clifford Norris as "unexplained and incomprehensible".

Recommendation 46.23 states that there can be no excuses for such a series of errors, failures and lack of direction and control. Each failure was compounded. Failure to acknowledge and to detect errors resulted in them being effectively concealed. The second investigation:

> attempted to salvage the situation and had no criticism of the investigation by Mr Mellish. Indeed it was managed with imagination and skill.

Management of the Major Incident Room (MIR)

In the Yorkshire Ripper case, Byford criticised the amount of "unprocessed information" in the MIR. Bilton (2003) comments that the Byford team found *"major flaws in the inquiry and its management in total disarray"* (p. 302). The Byford team found a lack of "standing back and reviewing evidence" in the Ripper investigation. The Milgarth Incident Room became overwhelmed and had the direct effect of frustrating the work of SIOs and junior detectives alike. The management of the flow of information into the MIR was the subject of concern in many of the inquiries. The Yorkshire Ripper case was the most glaring example of the failure to provide an adequate database or system to link cases or identify killers across force boundaries. This was also true with the Maxwell, Hogg and Harper murders and the Soham case. The Lawrence report stated that the MIR was "inadequately staffed" (recommendation 46.14) and that the incident room was not supervised by responsible and trained staff. The report felt that this may account for the many delays apparent in the processing of information reaching the investigation team.

Information Management

Lord Laming stated that the management of information is paramount to the success of an investigation. Child Protection Teams should have an effective Child Protection database and IT management system. Byford commented that the MIR in the Yorkshire Ripper case was "overwhelmed by a welter of information". The Holmes system was an advance following the Yorkshire Ripper case but in cases such as the Soham inquiry it cannot cope with the volume of information generated in high volume cases.

Individual Investigative Strategy Failures

In the Climbie Investigation Lord Laming states that an investigation should have begun straight away after Police were notified of the original problems and numerous detailed investigative leads were not adopted by the investigators. They were criticised by Lord Laming for not taking the basic steps required in a major investigation and therefore vital evidence was lost. In the Soham case the HMIC report stated that there could have been a greater sense of urgency and they commented that the

> good momentum achieved by the initial officers dealing with the incident could have been consolidated.

The report stated that high priority leads were not acted on for more than one week. There was an inability to appreciate the golden hour's value of the information generated by the enquiry. Senior officers failed to act on valuable evidential leads gathered by officers on the ground. The HMIC report stated that the first SIO refused to deploy extra officers on the night the victims went missing. The report states that

> there was a lack of clarity around who was running the investigation and Mr Beck was unable to maintain control and knowledge of the overall strategic direction of the investigation.

Many witnesses are naturally unfriendly to police enquires and the SIO has to draw up strategies accordingly. In many of the cases mentioned here witnesses were reluctant to come forward and this necessitated the SIO seeking a pro-active use of recruiting informants and seeking intelligence from other means.

In the Macpherson Report Chapter 19 refers to the handling of witnesses. Paragraph 19.41 states

> There was an overriding need in this investigation to turn information into evidence and to turn reluctant witnesses into willing ones in order to obtain the fullest possible information and evidence. There is no doubt that the investigation team felt rightly that there were witnesses who were saying less than they actually knew. Most if not all of these witnesses were young people, sometimes with a basic antipathy to the police. In these circumstances a tactful and sensitive approach to witnesses was needed.

The review panel looking at the Damilola Taylor case found in Recommendation 3.8.9 that the evidential opportunities that presented themselves during the investigation were correctly identified and acted upon. Recommendation 3.8.10 states that one potential source of evidence, the mobile telephones were not properly pursued and the acquisition of potential evidence deriving from the footwear of one suspect. In the Shipman enquiry, Dame Smith comments that "it appears that (the) DI may have been looking for a motive rather than gathering evidence" (p. 49). Dame Smith comments that it was clear that the DI "did not think carefully about the information he had received from Mr. Loader, the Superintendent Registrar at Delfield. He did not test the validity of the statistics he was given" (p. 51). In Chapter 13 of her report on the Shipman inquiry she states that DI Smith did not progress the enquiry for 2 weeks at the start of April, then "there was a flurry of activity" (p. 93). DI Smith then in a discussion with Chief Superintendent Sykes stated that there was no foundation for the concerns expressed by the original complainant and the first police investigation was closed. Dame Janet states that DI Smith never understood the issues concerned., "never had a plan of action" (p. 134) and that he was allowed to close the investigation before it was complete. By not acting in the early part of April DI Smith failed to arrange an autopsy on Mrs. Aida Warburton's body.

Summary

Past inquiries can help inform present or future investigative strategies by providing best practice and highlighting potential pitfalls. There is a need to retain organisational learning from past inquiries to assist future generations of investigators. Table 2.1 shows the systematic failures repeated over the last 40 years. In the majority of cases researched, there were shortcomings in the resourcing and cross-checking capability of the MIR. This applies to both pre- and post-HOLMES incident rooms. The role of the MIR and Holmes since the Yorkshire Ripper case illustrates the progress that has been made although in the case of the Harper, Maxwell and Hogg murders the suspect was not within the system. In the report on the Stephen Lawrence case Lord MacPherson stated that the MIR was "inadequately staffed" (recommendation 46.14) and that the incident room was not supervised by responsible and trained staff.

But the review panel in the Taylor case commented (recommendation 6.5) that there were "demonstrable differences" between the police handling of the investigation of this case and that of the Stephen Lawrence case.

The issue of leadership among senior management teams and SIOs was discussed in the inquiries researched. The Byford report on the Yorkshire Ripper case states that "it was ACC's Oldfield failure to lead effectively which paved the way for the loss of confidence in and loyalty to his inquiry policies".

The inquiries have shown consistent themes including the fact that the wrong people were in charge of inquiries at critical stages of major enquires. Bad decisions as in the Lawrence case were compounded. Police must learn from these cases, the recurrence of the same themes over time causes concern. Similarly the unintended consequences shown must be monitored to ensure that the recommendations of inquiries do not become a burden in themselves.

REFERENCES

Adhami, E., & Browne, D. (1996). *Major Crime Enquiries: Improving Expert Support for Detectives*. UK: Police Research Group Special Interest Paper 9.

Bilton, M. (2003). *Wicked Beyond Belief*. Harper Collins.

IPOC (IPCC) Report on Poppi Worthington.

Irving, B., & Dunningham, C. (1993). *Human Factors in the Quality control of CID investigations and a review of training*. Research papers on Criminal Justice Studies.

Jones, D., Grieve, J., & Milne, B. (2008). The Case to Review Murder Investigations. *Policing, 2*(4), 470–480.

KIrby, S. (2013). *Effective Policing*. Palgrave Macmillan.

Nicol, C., Innes, M., Gee, D., & Feist, A. (2004). *Reviewing Murder Investigations: An Analysis of Progress Reviews from 6 Police Forces*. Online Report 25/04 UK.

NPCC Core Investigative Doctrine. library.college.police.uk/docs/acpo/Core-Investigative-Doctrine.pdf.

Orde., H, & Rea, D. (2017). *"Bear in Mind These Dead": The Omagh Bombing and Policing*. Belfast: Nicholson and Bass.

Smith, N., & Flanagan, C. (2000). *The Effective Detective: Identifying the Skills of an Effective SIO*. London: Police Research Group, Home Office, UK.

Reports

A Report on the Investigation by Cambridgeshire Constabulary into the
    Murders of Jessica Chapman and Holly Wells at Soham 4 August 2002
    HMIC Sir Ronnie Flanagan HMIC.
Sir William Macpherson Report on the Death of Stephen Lawrence CM 4261. 1
    February 1999 Stationary Office, UK.
The Damilola Taylor Murder Investigation Review: The Report of the Oversight
    Panel December 2002 Metropolitan Police, UK.
The Shipman Inquiry 2nd Report: The Police Investigation of 1998 (2003)
    Chairman Dame Janet Smith OBE HMSO.
The Victoria Climbie Report. https://www.gov.uk/government/publications/
    the-victoria-climbie.

CHAPTER 3

Good Practice Solving Factors

Mark Roycroft

Abstract The chapter illustrates the significance of the Senior Investigating Officers (SIOs) decision-making and management style. It identifies the key variables that solved the murder cases within the 166 cases researched. The seven broad solving themes and 41 solving factors help to explain how these major cases are dealt with. It highlights the importance of what the police do and how crucial the management of witnesses is to the success of inquiries. The selection of the correct solving factor for the inquiry being investigated is a crucial element to success. The positive and negative pressures within the separate investigations are identified. The SIOs management style was an important factor in the decision-making process and the inclusive approach was used by successful SIOs. The less successful SIOs had a more reactive style responding to events rather that anticipating them. The inclusive style and the prioritisation of lines of enquiry were significant inter-related with Holmes activity. The inclusive style encouraged the team to participate. The author explored how the type of case under investigation can influence the outcome of an investigation. Hostile witnesses, lack of

M. Roycroft (✉)
Open University, Milton Keynes, UK
e-mail: mark.roycroft@open.ac.uk

© The Author(s) 2019
M. Roycroft and J. Roach (eds.),
Decision Making in Police Enquiries and Critical Incidents,
https://doi.org/10.1057/978-1-349-95847-4_3

forensic opportunities and lack of passive data can all contribute to difficulties in a particular case. All of these can be outside the SIOs control. The SIO can only deal with the "witnesses they are given."

Keywords Decision making styles · Democratic · Innovative · Autocratic · Management by rote · Replicative behaviour · Good practice · Phasing of enquires · Good practice · Systematic management · Management style

This chapter is concerned with how the decision-makers' decision making style and choice of decisions solve high-profile cases. The chapter draws on the author's research of 166 murder cases and interviews with 34 Senior Investigating Officers (SIOs). Following analysis of these interviews and secondary analysis of the findings a total of 41 Solving Factors were identified. These cases were protracted and required a series of phases to maintain and preserve the investigation.

CONTRIBUTION OF INVESTIGATIVE PROCESSES AND SIO STYLE TO THE RESOLVING OF CRIMES

The Role of Experience

The SIOs were broken down into different groups according to their clear up rate i.e. the number of cases they solved during the research period. 11 SIOs had a 100% clear up rate the majority being "career detectives" i.e. they had been in the CID at each rank of their service. Compared to the SIOs in the "poor" category i.e. with a clear up rate less than 50% where the majority (6 out of 8) were transfers from uniform policing.

Successful SIOs were those who choose strategies in the early phase of the enquiry and had the ability to quickly make decisions. A period of initial activity was followed by a period of review. The "innovative" SIOs were creative and flexible in their decision-making processes and looked at all possible methods to help solve the crimes. They were consultative in their management of specialist teams and sought to use "the creative brain" of their respective teams. They in short brought a complete "tool kit" of management and investigative skills to their enquiries.

All of the successful SIOs indicated they used the following strategic themes (see Table 3.1)

- Witness management
- CCTV
- Forensic
- Intelligence and
- Investigative thinking (unique lines that the SIO introduced)
- Media

The use of "Investigative Thinking" (i.e. what the SIO themselves brought to the investigation) by the successful SIOs also reflects their wider decision-making process. The use of investigative thinking is predicted to increase solvability by 44 times. This concept relates to the hypothesis setting and verification processes that the SIO brought to the enquiry. The more systematic review of the evidence and information is more effective than simple application of options by rote and replicating previous practices without appreciating their discriminating power of analysis under different circumstances. This was used by 7 out of the 8 highly successful SIOs.

GOOD PRACTICE

Clarity of Leadership

The SIO needs to operate within a supportive environment with clear terms of reference. The lack of clarity resulting in blurred lines of responsibility can create unintended consequences in critical incidents (see the Damiola Taylor review on confusion around command structures). This can lead to blurred lines of responsibility and may over-complicate the line of command. Successful SIOs managed their teams well by hearing what they have to say and allowing them to volunteer their own ideas about the enquiry. They also managed upwards; keeping Senior Management Teams informed, similarly the SIO has to provide their team with a clear strategy whilst encouraging debate and ideas from the team. The investigative stage of decision-making requires the SIO to ensure that their strategy is understood and fully implemented by their team.

SPECIFIC SKILLS

Knowledge Requirements

The SIO needs a good knowledge of police procedure in major enquires and full awareness of the Holmes system as well as the MIRSAP protocol. Legal knowledge is important not only in the legal requirements for arrest and detention but also the wider legal context of the enquiry. The SIO must recognise the spirit of the law and what is acceptable before the Court and what possible defences may be offered by the defendant. Similarly the SIO must liaise with the Crown Prosecution Service (CPS) and be aware of their requirements. The SIOs must have knowledge of forensic techniques to conduct forensic management and what is needed at the scene and forensic opportunities through the investigation. This may involve setting a forensic strategy for arrests and searches as well as being aware of issues such as contamination and continuity of exhibits.

SYSTEMIC MANAGEMENT

For every additional investigative strategy used there is a doubling of the likelihood of solving cases. The key tactics are:

- investigative thinking,
- early witness strategy, and
- house to house enquiries.

By being proactive an SIO can reduce the length of an enquiry by up to 5 months.

Systematic and individual investigative strategy failures can be avoided by a rigorous review policy by an internal review group. This group should also play an important part in the continuous development of SIOs ensuring that they comprehend the solving factors and processes for dealing with major cases.

Ensuring implementation of the SIOs strategy is perhaps the hardest part of an SIOs responsibility. The "co ordinated implementation process" is vital to the success of an enquiry. An SIO must deal with a complex set of heuristics to evaluate the potential solving factors. The development of hypothesis and the actions necessary to implement the policy are indica-tors of the more systematic approach taken by successful SIOs.

Decision-Making Styles of Investigators

The research evidence revealed four main types of management style (see Appendix 2):

- Democratic
- Innovative
- Autocratic
- Management by rote

About a third were "democratic" (32.2%) with innovative SIOs representing 16.1% and autocratic 29%. Management by rote represented 22.6% of the total number of SIOs management style. The highest clear up rate was for innovative SIOs at 85.4% with "democratic" SIOs at 79.5%.

Table 3.1 below shows the high number of individual solving fac-tors used by SIO's during the 166 cases researched by the author. The management of witnesses was seen to be the second most highly used solving factor, reflecting the importance of witness to cases. The use of Forensic material unsurprisingly was the most frequently suc-cessful solving factor. The use of passive data including telephone data and electronic messaging was a further frequently successful factor. It is important to note the importance of what the Police themselves did during an enquiry and this is illustrated by the high number of strat-egies used by investigating officers including covert surveillance and pro active methods techniques, house to house enquiries and using intelligence by local officers. The "Investigating Thinking" used by Senior Investigating Officers was a significant factor and reflected the importance of what the SIO does during an enquiry. The "Arrest strategy" used by officers also illustrated the careful planning needed during investigations to ensure that the sequencing of phases of the enquiry were co ordinated, i.e suspects were arrested in the correct order to ensure maximum evidential opportunities. The use of Police Intelligence databases and informants demonstrated the importance of Intelligence gathering and its analysis.

Table 3.1 Frequency with which strategies and tactics used

	No of times used successfully	% of total	No of times considered by SIO
Police			
Witness mgt	54	32.5	166
Investigative thinking	31	18.7	38
Covert techniques	18	10.2	41
Local officers	17	9.6	130
House to house	17	10.2	166
Proactive survey	16	9.0	38
Arrest strategy	12	7.2	62
Linked cases	5	3.0	166
FLO	4	2.4	166
Reward	3	1.8	102
Anniversary appeal	2	1.2	166
Holmes	2	1.2	142
Polsa	2	1.2	89
Post charge strategy	1	0.6	34
Legal			
Consult with CPS	10	6	166
Identity parades	17	10.2	89
Witness albums	1	0.6	76
Immunity	1	0.6	1
Technical			
Forensic techniques	62	37.8	156
CCTV footage	42	25.6	128
Phone analysis	45	27.1	123
Private CCTV	3	1.8	22
Recovery murder weapon	10	6.0	141
Use of E Fit	6	3.6	22
ANPR	1	0.6	45
Intelligence			
Police Intelligence databases	48	22.9	16
Use of informants	17	10.2	6
Use of analysis	9	5.4	52
Use of financial analysis	8	2	166
			32
Non police experts			
NCF/NPIA (now NCA)	10	4.6	54
Liaison outside	7	4.2	38
Agencies	5	3.6	165
Pathology	4	2.4	15
Behavioural profiling	1	0.6	7
Geographical profiling			

(continued)

Table 3.1 (continued)

	No of times used successfully	% of total	No of times considered by SIO
Media			
Media generally	12	3.0	117
Crimewatch	1	0.6	7
Crimestoppers	1	0.6	67
Suspect behaviour			
Confessions	4	2.4	4
Dying declaration	2	1.2	2
Interviews	4	2.4	166

Total = 515

MANAGEMENT STYLE

The type of management style and the ability of the SIO to constantly review his/her strategy are critical. There is a need to assess future SIOs for their potential decision-making processes prior to their initial deployment. The ability to choose the correct theme of murder case at the right time is one of the key elements of success. Democratic management of the MIT emerged as a critical trait along with the ability to manage the different phases of the enquiry over long periods of time. The SIO has to have the ability to constantly review all the information and potential evidence before him or her, be open to feedback from the team and have the ability to use "the collective brain of the team". Key to the successful charging of suspects is a flexible and creative approach, along with being proactive and evaluating alternative interpretations as evidence amasses.

Central to effective decision-making is the idea of a diagnostic inclination in which the SIO brings skills and disposition to approach the investigation in a systematic and analytic fashion. The SIO diagnoses an unfamiliar situation and designs a course of action to deal with it. The heuristics that SIOs develop enable them to utilise a framework to understand complex investigations. This enables SIOs to order their decision-making. By systemising the decision-making process the SIO can start to prioritise lines of enquiry and order the phasing of the case before them. Diagnostic inclination embodies a need to assess incoming information, quickly reviewing all information and prioritising certain actions.

This systematic approach to investigation reduced the time taken and the more pro active SIOs reduced the time taken by up to 5 months. The good SIO needs an ability to balance all the needs of the enquiry simultaneously while responding quickly to ongoing issues within the case.

SPECIFIC INVESTIGATIVE STRATEGIES

The selection of the correct solving factors for the right theme of murder was shown as important for the success of an enquiry. The research showed that the successful SIOs indicated that they used the following strategic themes

- Witness management
- CCTV
- Forensic
- Intelligence
- Investigative thinking
- Media strategy

WITNESS MANAGEMENT

Better management of witnesses may lead to more convictions at court and perhaps more likelihood of suspects being picked out on identity parades. The management of witnesses over the lifespan of an enquiry is important and The Trials Unit (the unit that looks after witnesses at the Central Criminal Court, London) felt that this reflected the difficulties with witnesses in some cases who changed their minds under pressure from family or indirectly from the suspects. This highlights the need for the police to protect and monitor witnesses. This can place an enormous strain on police resources which SIOs need to be aware of and take into account.

DECISION-MAKING TECHNIQUES BY THE SIO

The SIO needs to be able to identify and apply the appropriate solving factor as well as the simultaneous maintenance of multiple solving factors as critical to the success of an enquiry. The need to construct a case with up to 12 potential solving factors at one time is a key element of success. The SIO needs to:

- Work through the evaluative stage in the decision frame employing a creative management style and prioritising the initial actions
- Ensure all lines of enquiry are adequately resourced
- Ensure the policy is fully implemented
- Ensure that all the Holmes (the database used by Murder Teams in the UK) actions relate to the SIOs strategy are executed
- Ensure all strategies are articulated in the SIO decision log.

Crucial decision-making skills include:

- Constant review of the enquiry
- Selection of the correct solving factors for particular types of enquiry
- holding regular office meetings to listen to the views of members of the team while retaining overall responsibility for decision making.

The recording of the SIOs thought process in their decision/Policy logs enables an accurate record to be established of the progress of the enquiry. It helps to explain to a court or review team why certain decisions were made at particular times. The policy log should act as a chronological description of the progress of the enquiry and should reflect the SIOs thought process.

How Findings Link to Decision-Making Theories

The research has shown that the SIOs use selected "triggers" and professional intuition to determine their decision-making processes. The SIO is concerned with the social context of the crime and filling the gaps in the information gathering stages, partly to identify the theme of the murder (i.e. its class or type). The successful SIOs tended to avoid replicated decision-making and tailored their decision-making to the type of crime being investigated rather than a generic template. The final deliberative stage of differentiated alternatives led to the selection of solving factors by reviewing the decision process. As Simon (1945) stated "decision-makers reduce information processing demands by constructing limited representations of options". Experts can use their experience to frame situations rapidly, as SIOs do by framing meaningful patterns and events. Naturalistic Decision Making (NDM) models assume that the decision situation is usually embedded within a broader

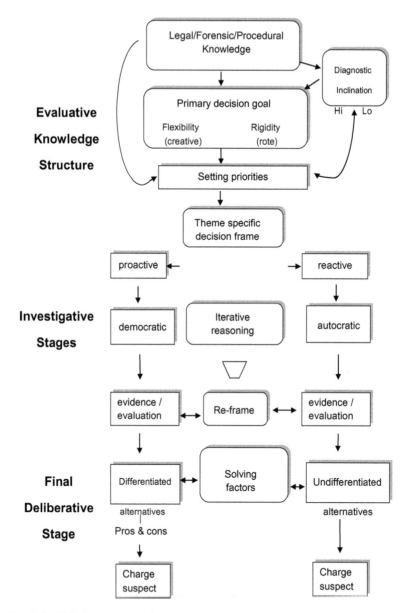

Fig. 3.1 Full decision model

environmental and organisational context. Adaptive expertise entails a deep comprehension of the conceptual structure of the problem domain. Once there appears to be other issues or risks or there are unreliable assumptions then the "correcting" stage is entered where more information needs to be collected. This stage requires the collection of additional data to resolve ambiguity. The decision nodes will be activated when enough knowledge is acquired. Metacognitive skills are needed in "the interpretative process of evaluating and revising assumptions".

Figure 3.1 suggests two routes through the decision-making process of an investigation. The right-hand route proposes a pathway drawing on procedural knowledge and past experience in a reactive manner and applying rote, by the book process. The alternative pathway is one in which the SIO is more creative and is able to differentiate the potential value of the available solving factors. The evaluative knowledge structure happens when the primary decision goal is moderated by diagnostic inclinations and the style of the SIO. At the investigative stage there is a funneling of information. Ensuring implementation of the SIOs strategy at this stage is the hardest part of the SIO's responsibilities. Most investigations require a co ordinated implementation process. This stage concerns the procedural features involved in the investigation with a more complex set of heuristics weighing up the pros and cons to evaluate the potential information to focus on the solving factors.

The chapter has illustrated the significance of the SIOs decision-making and management style. It has identified the key variables that solved the murder cases within the 166 cases researched. The seven broad solving themes and 41 solving factors help to explain how these major cases are dealt with. It highlights the importance of what the police do and how crucial the management of witnesses is to the success of inquiries. The selection of the correct solving factor for the inquiry being investigated is a crucial element to success. The positive and negative pressures within the separate investigations were identified.

The SIOs management style was an important factor in the decision-making process and the inclusive approach was used by successful SIOs. The less successful SIOs had a more reactive style responding to events rather that anticipating them. The inclusive style and the prioritisation of lines of enquiry were significant inter-related with Holmes activity. The inclusive style encouraged the team to participate.

REFERENCE

Simon, H. A. (1945). *Administrative Behavior*. New York: Free Press.

CHAPTER 4

Innate Reasoning and Critical Incident Decision-Making

Robin Bryant

Abstract The author describes the theory behind intuitive and analytical decision making during investigations. Forms of reasoning are described (including their limitations) together with a brief overview of what the fields of neuropsychology and evolutionary psychology might be able to contribute to our understanding. We often make decisions based on a serial assessment of information and we choose the first available workable option that appears to satisfy our requirements. Decisions during major incidents often have to be made in quick time by exercising swift judgement by choosing between options (including not to act). Inevitably, complex situations have to be simplified in the human mind with the number of options considered at any one time severely limited and inferences rapidly drawn. Heuristics are often employed to facilitate this, which whilst often effective are also linked with a number of well-known cognitive biases.

R. Bryant (✉)
School of Law and Criminal Justice, Canterbury Christ Church University,
Canterbury, UK
e-mail: robin.byrant@canterbury.ac.uk

© The Author(s) 2019   47
M. Roycroft and J. Roach (eds.),
Decision Making in Police Enquiries and Critical Incidents,
https://doi.org/10.1057/978-1-349-95847-4_4

Keywords Reasoning · Evolutionary psychology · Heuristics ·
Cognitive biases and decision making · Drawing inferences in decision
making

INTRODUCTION

During the policing of a critical incident, and despite all the technology available, it is still people and not machines that make most of the important decisions. Police officers attempt to make sense of the circumstances that confront them, respond to developments and take control by making decisions using the most powerful and adept tool available to them: their brains. This chapter examines some of the innate forms of reasoning that police officers employ to make decisions during critical incidents. However, from the outset it should be acknowledged that reasoning is but one element within an individual or group's decision-making repertoire during a critical incident. There is a widely accepted consensus within policing research that competent decision-making involves a combination of both general cognitive ability and domain-specific (e.g. occupational) understanding and skills, in which reasoning will play a major part, but only a part. We also limit this chapter to a discussion of the 'how' of innate reasoning within decision-making and say little on the 'why' or 'when'.

It is important to note that even within policing itself there are probably distinctly different forms of decision-making at work, and hence generalities concerning reasoning might be difficult to make. For example, Eyre and Alison (2010, p. 77) claim that 'investigative decision making is a specialist domain and some factors may pertain specifically or even exclusively to investigative decision making [...]'. We will also draw a distinction between police decision-making when it is made (is able to be made) more deliberately and collectively rather than in a split second by an individual deciding alone. When the latter involves potentially life-threatening consequences then the decision-making might well be made by necessity in a much more instinctive way. It is also the case that police decision-making often has unique constraints (for example, the maintenance of moral authority and legitimacy) which should make us cautious of assuming that research findings in even similarly 'clinician' based occupations will necessary also apply to policing.

Discussions in the literature concerning the nature of decision-making often make a distinction between the way things are (descriptive models) and the way things ought to be (normative models). The descriptive models set out the cognitive and other processes by which people actually make decisions in practice, for example, by observing that we make decisions based on a serial (not parallel) assessment of information; that we often choose the first available workable option that appears to satisfy our requirements and that we tend to concentrate on improving options, not looking for alternatives. 'Prospect theory'[1] is a good example of a descriptive model that provides a comprehensive description of the typical behaviour of people making decisions (in terms of risk-taking and risk-aversion). However, descriptive models also very often point to the shortcomings of human decision-making 'in the wild' (for example, the alleged widespread occurrence of cognitive biases in decision-making). Normative models on the other hand have a more 'scientific' flavour and often evoke rational choice theory, formal logic (e.g. syllogisms), a priori probability assessment (e.g. Bayesian conditional likelihoods) and adaptations of economic models such as expected utility.[2] It is easy to gain the spurious impression that normative models always offer the better approach to competent decision-making during critical incidents but as we illustrate in this chapter, this is not necessarily the case. This impression that normative is 'good' and descriptive is 'bad' might have arisen from the inappropriate application of organising principles derived from normative theories to descriptive ones (Mellers 1996) and this could also account for an apparent preoccupation with human cognitive errors in decision-making. Eyre and Alison (2007, pp. 212–216) draw a distinction between 'traditional, naturalistic and pragmatic approaches to decision-making' within critical incidents although they note that 'in a bid to draw distinctions between different schools of thought in decision-making theory, it is possible that a false dichotomy has been created' (ibid., p. 214). The concept of 'bounded rationality' provides a good example of how the possibly false dichotomy between normative approaches and the reality of decision-making can be bridged. A now famous essay of Herbert Simon[3] sets out the argument

---

[1] An economic theory developed by Kahneman and Tversky in the late 1970s.

[2] A method of assessing the likelihood of each event and calculated an overall expected value.

[3] 'A Behavioral Model of Rational Choice' first published in 1955 in the *Quarterly Journal of Economics* and subsequently in Simon's book *Models of Man: Social and Rational.*

that the apparently rational process of determining the best decision by assessing every possible feasible choice and calculating the costs and benefits of each (a normative approach) is itself a prohibitively costly undertaking. In reality, Simon argued, people adopt an alternative approach of setting a threshold where the outcome is 'good enough'[4] and the first choice that meets or exceeds the threshold will be the one chosen (even if it happens not to be the 'best' in terms of expected value).

In practice, observational and other research have identified significant differences in decision-making strategies adopted by law enforcement officers during critical incidents (e.g. Sharps 2010). Two distinct clusters of decision-making strategies can be discerned, which whilst neither mutually exclusive nor exhaustive are sufficiently different to justify drawing distinctions. One cluster involves decision-making strategies which might be termed 'intuitive'[5] with strategies adopted quickly, with little conscious effort, based on recognition of the situation, using visual and other cues. Intuitive approaches tend to be employed by the more expert practitioner, often using a combination of learning through experience and heuristics (see later). Lipshitz and Ben Shaul (1997) also highlight the difference that 'novices will deliberate about which option to select whilst experts will deliberate about what is going on in the situation'. The second cluster, which we term 'analytical' requires more time, often involves applying a linear set of rules (for example, 'Standard Operating Procedures'), is more consciously analytical in nature and can appear to the novice as the 'safer' option.

Reasoning

Both 'intuitive' and 'analytical' decision-making strategies will include at least some element of innate or conscious 'reasoning'—a process within the mind of a person whereby he or she expects to arrive at reliable

---

[4] See the concept of 'satificing'.

[5] We use the words 'innate', 'instinct' and 'intuition' rather loosely and interchangeably in this chapter although it is acknowledged that differences between the concepts are often important. 'Innate' normally refers to the abilities that we inherit; 'instinct' is often taken as an innate automatic behaviour that is reflexive in nature whereas 'intuition' is a somewhat wider term referring to an unconscious ability to 'know' (which might result from learning, experience or innate traits).

insights. Reasoning in decision-making is often utilised to differentiate between cause and effect, to predict the consequences of taking or not taking an action, to establish what has motivated another individual to behave in a certain way, to infer the existence of some effect or phenomenon and to challenge the hypotheses or reasoning of others. Often the process of reasoning is several cognitive steps removed from consciously and deliberately taking a decision. For example, police officers very often request further knowledge during critical incidents and may not even be aware of the explicit reasons why they need the specific information but will have a sense that it will aid decision-making in some way. In many cases they will be right.

Reason underpins a person's judgement,[6] defined as the 'set of evaluative and inferential processes that people have at their disposal and can draw on in the process of making decisions' (Koehler and Harvey 2004, p. xv). Judgment involves reasoning in practical, non-abstract circumstances and gives rise to action and hence in police critical decision-making is of particular importance. However, sound (valid and reliable) reasoning does not necessarily in, and of itself, lead to the 'correct' judgement being made. There are a number of reasons why this might be, including on strictly logical grounds (reasoning has led to a sound argument being employed, but founded on invalid assumptions and hence leading to skewed judgement) but also the somewhat more obvious problem of the limitations in the information available in a critical incident. We might also reason to the 'right' judgement but then make a different, wrong decision for physiological or psychological reasons or because of the adverse influence of 'group think'. Blood glucose levels might play a part in making our decisions more intuitive and less deliberate (Orquin and Kurzban 2016) and stress when making decisions in emergency circumstances can lead to either increasing the likelihood of making the wrong decision or (in the case of moderate stress) improving decision-making capability (Starckea and Branda 2012). Light levels, noise, temperature of the environment, adrenaline levels in the body (and the counter-acting neuropeptides) might all influence how a police officer's reasoning affects their judgement.

---

[6]A term often employed in police critical incident training.

NEUROPSYCHOLOGY, DECISION-MAKING AND REASONING

Although it risks stating the obvious, it is worth at this point reminding ourselves that, at the most fundamental level, the reasoning that underpins decision-making in critical incidents is a case of the people concerned using their brains. The human mind is of immense complexity and uses over 20% of the body's energy intake, whilst only occupying approximately 3% of its mass. They are thought to be over 85 billion neurons in the human brain with 125 billion synapses in the cerebral cortex alone, a number at least 1000 times the number of stars in our galaxy (Garrett 2014). In many respects it is a very 'costly' organ for humans to have, but as with all other organs of the body it was the process of evolution that gave rise to the brain and the mind within. The mind was 'designed' (by natural selection) to maximise the number of copies of the genes that gave rise to its existence. Natural selection is a process that takes place over millions of years and our brains are the product of adaptation for gene transmission (they have been 'hardwired'). Neurologically our brains today are much the same as human brains in prehistoric times. It follows that although prehistoric people no doubt had their own 'critical incidents' to deal with the brains we share with them have not been adapted for new phenomena such emailed information arriving on a smartphone. It is no surprise then to discover that in terms of the functional specialisation of different parts of the brain it is unlikely that there exists a specific 'module' for 'reasoning'. Instead the traits that we usually consider examples of 'reasoning' are more likely closely associated with cognitive functions such as language. Logical processes (such as forms of deduction) might also involve the 'co-option' of special hardwired inference rules about the natural world (Pinker 2003, p. 32). More recently Donoso et al. (2014) have used the results of neuroimaging and brain imaging to propose analgorithmic model of human reasoning,[7] neurologically situated within the prefrontal cortex (PFC) part of the brain. The PFC would appear to have a track between regions of the PFC which calculates probabilistic inferences to 'arbitrate' between staying with an initial adopted problem-solving strategy, reverting to previous learned strategies

---

[7] Note that the form of 'reasoning' used in the experiments and subsequent modelling involved participants searching using trial and error methods for 3-digit combinations of numbers (Donoso et al. 2014, p. 1481).

or switching to a new strategy. At the same time, a second track between two regions of the PFC assesses the reliability of two or three alternative strategies and decides whether to 'run' with an alternative or look for new strategies. The interaction of the two tracks determines the outcome of either accepting or rejecting a possible new strategy.

EVOLUTIONARY PSYCHOLOGY, DECISION-MAKING AND REASONING

In this section we examine the contribution evolutionary psychology might make to a greater understanding of how police officers reason when decisions are made, particularly when intuitive response are made during critical incidents. Evolutionary psychology is defined by Kenrick et al. (2003, p. 4) as 'the study of cognitive, affective, and behavioural mechanisms as solutions to recurrent adaptive problems'. A psychological trait is 'adaptive' when its existence leads to an increase in 'fitness': that is it will tend to increase the likelihood of future generations in terms of offspring or genes. 'Adaptive problems' are those presented by the environment at the time of adaptation (the 'environment' includes competing humans as well as the natural world).

It should be noted however that evolutionary psychology does not claim to provide an explanation for all intuitive decision-making and neither would any serious scientist claim that we are 'programmed' by our genes to reason, judge and decide in certain ways (e.g. see Roach and Pease 2013). Clearly, learning through experience is an important contributory factor in the success of our reasoning when making decisions. However, even the ability to learn from our previous actions (or indeed, from the behaviour of others) when reasoning has evolved as a consequence of our evolutionary survival and not simply because it is a 'good thing' in its own right. As Hammerstein and Stevens (2012, p. 5) explain, 'the evolutionary preparedness of learning is thus fundamental to understanding mechanisms of decision-making'.

One reason why evolutionary psychology has been invoked in trying to understand decision-making is that our intuitive reasoning under uncertainty and risk has been shown not to follow rational classical forms, such as expected utility. In many cases humans[8] make intuitive decisions that contradict those that would be predicted from rational

---

[8] And some other species.

choice theory (Kahneman and Twersky 2000). However, this does not mean that our intuitive decision-making is without reason or in some way 'random': rather, there is an 'ecological rationality' too much of our innate reasoning. Mata et al. (2012), explain that this rationality can be seen in the way in which our decision processes have been adapted to particular environments; in the fact that in many circumstances simple decision strategies are as good as, if not better, than more complex ones and finally that we are adept at modifying our strategies to match the context. The particular environments for which our innate decision-making processes are adapted is our 'ancestral' environment, technically towards the end of Pleistocene era (a physical environment that was much like the modern day African savannah). Everyone alive today in the world shares a common ancestor in the last 100 generations and in many respects we are indistinguishable from our common ancestors from 50 to 60,000 years ago. Evolutionary psychologists argue that many of our instinctive ways of making decisions are rooted in this common ancestral 'hunter gatherer' past and are the product of evolutionary adaptation by natural and other forms of selection.[9] These instinctive forms of decision-making are a consequence of our success as a species in solving the practical problems of survival (finding and consuming food, avoiding premature death and successfully reproducing). As a corollary, the intuitive forms of reasoning that underpin our decisions are similarly adapted for Darwinian fitness payoffs (food, safety, mating opportunities and developing social bonds) for the purpose of increasing the likely number of surviving offspring that we foster. Thus selection promotes adaptively successful reasoning and not necessarily the 'right' decisions (when placed against non-adaptive criteria), or ones that are consistent from time to time, or indeed ones that are always altruistic in nature.

There are clear examples of adaptive decision-making strategies in our response to situations that might prove costly in terms of our Darwinian fitness, namely those that threaten our personal survival. One such strategy is the so-called 'smoke alarm principle'. Obviously, real smoke alarms are designed to activate when fire or smoke is detected. Less obvious is that are two important errors to consider in the design of smoke alarms: one is that there is always the possibility of 'false positives', that is the detector will incorrectly go off but there is really no fire or smoke;

---

[9] Adaptation also occurs by other means such as genetic mutation but we omit the details here.

the second is that the detector will fail to warn us of a genuine fire, a 'false negative'.[10] The false positives might be irritating to a home owner but the false negatives have potentially much more serious consequences. Hence smoke alarms are engineered as far as possible to minimise the likelihood of false negatives but the designers are less concerned about the probability of false positives. Similarly, in terms of our ancestral 'reasoning' the error in mistaking a stick for a snake has far less adverse fitness implications than erroneously deciding that a snake is a stick: in this case we are primed (biased) in our rapid intuitive decision-making to minimise the false negative, not the false positive (Johnson et al. 2013). In more general terms, we have probably evolved not only to look for the option with the greatest return (for example, high calorie foods) but on many occasions (particularly ones that are life-threatening) to avoid those with the greatest loss in terms of gene transmission (our continued existence). It is interesting to note, for example, that in those small number of occasions when police Authorised Firearms Officers in England and Wales use potentially lethal force (in about two to six incidents per year from a total of 10,000 or so operations in which firearms are authorised) IPCC reports suggest that on almost all occasions the use of force was justified on the grounds of immediate threat to the AFO's life and whilst in positions of close physical proximity to a suspect.[11]

In terms of reasoning in particular, whilst it is unlikely that adaptation through natural selection would have favoured the development of explicitly more abstract forms of reasoning (such as 'deduction') research with infants does suggest that we have innate ways of 'working things out'. These inherited forms of reasoning might well 'piggy back' on our innate understanding of the predictable ways objects behave (for example, that no two objects can occupy the same space), how forces act upon objects, how projectiles move[12] and the differentiation between colours (identifying harmful foods). It is possible that the rules that govern space, time, the animal kingdom and plants are 'co-opted' as the basis for making other (more abstract) inferences. In more general terms, evolved forms of reasoning probably include the ability to categorise, to monitor

[10]'False positives' and 'false negatives' are parallels of the Type 1 and Type 2 errors encountered in other examples of testing, for example presumptive testing for the presence of illegal drugs or explosives.

[11]Rather than, say, on the grounds of a direct threat to a hostage's life or safety.

[12]In ancestral terms presumably this was important for the ability to hunt and to fight.

frequencies, to detect when objects often occur together (association), to notice when one thing is contingent upon another and some attributes of cause and effect.

At least some of the inherited reasoning at our disposal appears to be specifically deontic[13] in nature (it is concerned with working out what we may, must or must not do) involving the judging of permissions, obligations and prohibitions. An example of deontic reasoning that evolved for clear survival purposes is the 'logic' of the detection of cheating (that is, to spot whether another member of the hunter-gatherer group has an unfair share of food or mates). When participating in social exchange we agree to deliver a benefit conditionally—that is, conditional on the other person doing what we require in return (reciprocating). Humans are ancestrally predisposed to detect, engage in, and reason effectively about social exchange. We use a 'social contract algorithm' (a set of rules) to work out whether to exchange or not (with a sub-routine of the algorithm devoted to identifying 'cheaters', Cosmides et al. 2010, p. 298).

A significant area within decision-making research is concerned with the extent to which people are innately accurate at judging the probability of an event. On the surface, the trait of being able to estimate the likelihood of events with adaptive significance, based on similar occurrences in the past, should be an ability that we innately possess. Particularly adaptive would be an innate ability to judge how likely one event is, given that another event has already occurred (a compound probability). If further relevant information becomes available during decision-making this might also be reasonably expected to have some influence on our estimates of the likelihood of certain consequences following. In formal probability theory these compound and conditional probabilities are calculated a priori using Bayes' Theorem, a mathematical formula.[14] However, when people are confronted with problems of calculating compound probabilities in laboratory settings using decimal expressions of probability they often arrive at the wrong estimates for the likelihood. This includes professional medical clinicians, despite the fact that they have been given the all the information required (Hoffrage and Gigerenzer 1998). Clearly, Bayes' Theorem does not appear to be hardwired in our brains as a consequence of evolution.

---

[13] That is, relating to duty and obligation.

[14] Technically, if A and B are events then Bayes' Theorem states that the conditional probability of A given B (written as $P(A|B)$) is calculated using $[P(B|A)P(A)]/P(B)$.

In 1973 Kahneman and Twersky observed that 'in making predictions and judgments under uncertainty, people do not appear to follow the calculus of chance or the statistical theory of prediction' (Kahneman and Tversky 1973, p. 237 cited in Meder and Gigerenzer 2014, p. 130). However, it has since been discovered that when such likelihood problems are recast in terms of frequencies rather than probabilities and presented in more visual ways then the performance of individuals significantly improves (Hoffrage et al. 2015). We do not appear to instinctively reason in terms of the probability of single events in space and time.[15] Instead, humans do appear often intuitively capable of making reasonably accurate estimates of the likelihood of events based on proportions of frequencies in the past. Pease and Roach have recently suggested that police decision-making is more aligned to Bayesian thinking than a consequentialist approach, for example 'if this, then this and this are likely' is a common way police test and modify their hypotheses in a criminal investigation (Pease and Roach 2017).

HEURISTICS, COGNITIVE BIASES AND DECISION-MAKING

The 'heuristic' is a form of decision-making that uses simple 'rules of thumb' reasoning to solve complex problems (Mousavi and Gigerenzer 2014, p. 5). Heuristics can (particularly when applied in ecologically sound circumstances which require rapid decision-making) perform as well, and often better than more formal methods.[16] We inherit a set of heuristics as a consequence of adaptation by natural and other forms of selection. Characteristically these heuristics are 'fast and frugal'; 'fast' in that they do not consciously use complicated calculations and 'frugal' because they only use some of the information available. None-the-less they often produce accurate judgements. Remarkably, heuristics do not necessary trade off accuracy for speed and in many cases more information and computation do not necessarily lead to better decisions (Todd and Gigerenzer 1999).

An example of heuristic often used during police decision-making is the 'anchoring and adjustment' heuristic. This is the technique of

[15] Indeed, as Pinker (2003) observes, in terms of human understanding, in many circumstances calculating the probability of a specific occurrence of an event in time may not make much sense.

[16] However, they can also lead us seriously astray.

starting with a relatively simple working hypothesis that fits the known facts and adjusting the hypothesis as new information emerges. A number of other heuristics that are likely to be instinctively employed as reasoning[17] in critical incident decision-making. These include the 'representative' (or 'representativeness') heuristic: how typical is something of the overall set of such things? For example, are the actions of this person the behaviour expected of somebody who has committed a particular crime? There is also the 'satisficing' heuristic: search through and look at the alternative decisions that are immediately available, reason on their consequences and take the first that meets immediate needs. Finally, many readers will be familiar with the 'availability' heuristic (something that readily comes to mind is more likely to be more important) which is particularly likely to be employed when confronted with information overload.

However, one person's heuristic can be another's cognitive bias. As Brighton and Gigerenzer (2012, p. 7) observe, heuristics have now become widely associated with 'shoddy mental software', and deemed to be inferior to more formal analytical methods. Snook and Cullen, in reviewing the literature, note that a number of authorities argue that 'the use of heuristics by police officers is thought to produce reasoning errors that contribute to criminal investigative failures [...]' (Snook and Cullen 2009, p. 71). Cognitive biases, possibly leading to a 'wrong' decision[18] appear to be pervasive (see, for example, Gilovich et al. 2002). An example of a cognitive bias within police decision-making is so-called 'tunnel vision' or 'investigative bias'; the tendency that can lead police investigators to 'focus on one suspect or investigative theory, select and filter information and evidence, whilst ignoring or supressing information and evidence that may lead to another suspect or theory' (Salet and Terpstra 2013, p. 43). In 2006 it was estimated that since the advent of DNA evidence there had been over 150 post-conviction exonerations of people that were originally judged to be guilty in the US (Findley and Scott 2006). A common feature in many of these miscarriages of justice was the inadvertent use of tunnel vision (ibid) where a suspect was identified

---

[17] Normally implicitly.

[18] In terms of experimentation, the 'wrong' decision is often choosing an option that contradicts a rational judgement of economic gain or the correct mathematical assessment of probability. Note however that a cognitive bias does not by necessity lead to a wrong judgement or decision.

at the outset and then the investigation focussed on this person, selecting and assessing information as it came in through the distorted lens of supposed guilt.

There are a number of other cognitive biases of particular relevance to police decision-making, including the 'feature positive effect'[19] (the tendency to experience difficulty processing non-occurrences); the 'confirmatory bias' (unconsciously looking for evidence that supports a pre-existing schema or hypothesis),[20] the 'hindsight bias'[21] (distortions of memory leading to post hoc changes of likelihood estimates), the 'availability bias' (how easily previous similar examples come to mind) and finally the 'anchoring bias'[22] (the undue influence of the first eye-witness account, or a particularly emotionally impactive element of the incident).

Not unsurprisingly perhaps, many cognitive biases arose not by unfortunate 'accident' but for sound adaptive reasons: they are not 'quirks' but instead are echoes of innate decision-making strategies rooted in our ancestral past (Johnson et al. 2013, p. 474). Natural selection rewards rapid, efficient decision-making (including judgement) which is 'biased' towards increasing an individual's fitness within a given set of adaptive circumstances. Adaptation does not reward sound judgement per se.

The existence of these cognitive biases is well-recognised in the literature surrounding police decision-making during critical incidents. The UK's College of Policing for example, begins its advice on decision-making by warning against cognitive errors (College of Policing 2015).[23] In response, some police forces are attempting to introduce systematic ways of challenging cognitive bias in decision-making. For example, the Police Service of the Netherlands have engaged police 'contrarians' to offer alternative scenarios to police teams engaged in complex criminal investigations with a view of countering the cognitive bias due to tunnel

[19]We notice much more when things happen than when they don't. This can sometimes have serious implications in decision-making.

[20]The 'self-fulfilling prophecy', related to 'tunnel vision'. One way to counter this is ask the question: 'would the same facts fit an alternative explanation that points to the innocence, rather than guilt of the suspect?'

[21]'I knew it all along! A bias well-known to readers of detective fiction. The problem is that the bias can lead to inaccurate estimations of the likelihood of events.

[22]The unwelcome bedfellow of the anchoring and adjustment heuristic.

[23]The guidance does not define what constitutes sound reasoning.

vision. There remains an ongoing debate on whether professionals should use 'fully rational or heuristic-based strategies' (Eastwood et al. 2012, p. 458) in exercising judgement and making decisions.

DRAWING INFERENCES IN DECISION-MAKING

In this part of the chapter we look at the use of reasoning to draw an inference (for example, deriving conclusions) from the information available when making decisions during a critical incident. Within the multitude of ways that we draw inferences three particular 'canonical' forms of inferential reasoning are often identified in the literature: abduction,[24] induction and deduction.

In simple terms abductive reasoning is 'reasoning to the best available explanation' or deriving the most likely explanation that fits the observed facts, observations or assumptions we often employ abduction when we observe effects and infer causes. For example, if during a critical incident a police officer observes members of public running away from a particular location he or she is likely to infer that they were caused to do so by some event.[25] He or she considers other possible explanations[26] sufficiently unlikely in the circumstances to be discounted. Abductive reasoning is of particular importance in police critical incident decision-making for as Patokorpi (2007, p. 172) observes 'abduction comes to its own in the face of incomplete evidence and high uncertainty that are usually related to very rare or non-repeatable events and to the realm of the unique in general'.

In practice, abduction is often a sequential process with the outcome of each stage of abductive reasoning forming the basis of the next, although this sequence might occur in quick time. Abductive reasoning is also often 'non-monotonic' and dynamic in nature—the plausibility of an inference can increase or decrease as new information emerges or

---

[24] Note that 'abduction' in this context is not related to the criminal act of the same name; an unfortunate coincidence in the context of policing.

[25] Technically this is an example of 'selective abduction', a method of induction which chooses the most likely explanation from a set of likely explanations (Magnani 2001).

[26] There are an infinite number of other possibilities, some of vanishingly small likelihoods, e.g., all the members of the public were hypnotised at the same time and autosuggestion used.

is collected and the inference might be altered or even be abandoned altogether.

It should be noted however, that some forms of abductive reasoning are poorly understood (Schurz 2008, p. 205). It is not clear how much human perception (what we see, hear, smell) plays a part in the abductive reasoning process and 'visual abductive reasoning' might well be 'hard wired'. Hence police commanders might draw adductive inferences based as much on what they hear and see in the here and now (mediated through culture, personal experience and other influences) as they do on that which they read or remember. Further, just how we decide on the 'best explanation' when we reason abductively is far from clear: what, for example, are the 'salient' features that should be the basis for the inference?[27] It seems reasonable to assume that the best explanation is arrived at by reference to experience, an intuitive assessment of the likelihood of events, the police officer's knowledge of the people and locations involved. However, there is often also a form of Occam's Razor[28] at work where we accept the first 'best' explanation that we arrive at (although there is little research into how we do this). The problem might be that, as suggested by a number of commentators (e.g., Lipton 1991) the best available explanation may not always be good enough.

Deductive reasoning embraces a number of different forms of formal and informal logic, somewhat ambiguous in definition but essentially referring to the form of reasoning where a conclusion (the deduction) must necessarily follow if the assumptions (premises) are true. One of the most well-known forms of deduction is 'P implies Q; P is asserted to be true, so therefore Q must be true'.[29] An example of deduction is 'if a person is in one place then they cannot be in another at the same time'. Hence, if we observe a suspect on CCTV in real time outside St Pancras then it cannot be the same suspect that we are currently observing at Kings Cross. Most people follow these types of arguments easily when given in context using real-life examples. There are however, many other forms of deductive reasoning which are not familiar, in their abstract

---

[27] In reality by necessity there have to be shortcuts to finding explanations as with n 'dots' of information there are $2^n - (n+1)$ possible combinations of two or more possible explanations to methodically search through (Schum and Starace 1994, pp. 491–492).

[28] Occam's Razor, is a principle in philosophy that essentially advises that 'of all the possible explanations on offer, accept the simplest'.

[29] Known as 'modus ponens'.

forms, to most people. For example, a number of laboratory-based experiments seem to suggest that we are poor at intuitively applying the falsification rule[30] (that is, 'if P, then Q; not Q, therefore, not P') when reasoning, often looking instead for confirmation of an existing hypothesis.[31] However, people appear more likely to apply the falsification rule correctly when the same problem is recast in more ancestral terms of identifying social rule violation (Cosmides and Tooby 1992).

The strength of inference using deductive reasoning resides in its 'watertight' nature: the conclusion must by necessity follow from the suppositions.[32] However, the 'fatal flaw' with deduction (and particularly in policing contexts) is that we can only be completely certain about the truth of a conclusion if both the suppositions are correct and the deductive logic has been correctly applied. In some cases we will indeed be absolutely certain of the truth of the suppositions but then inferences derived in these circumstances tend towards the trivially obvious.

Inductive reasoning[33] takes a variety of forms, the most common being to generalise from specific occurrences that have common features to postulate a more general rule (to go from 'some' to 'all'). Familiar forms of inductive reasoning in policing include 'analogical reasoning' and 'case-based reasoning'. With case-based reasoning, decisions are made in critical incidents with reference (consciously or unconsciously) to previous similar (analogous) situations and often drawn from the experience of the individual. This form of inference can be thought of as a type of heuristic (see above) with the mental shortcut being: 'make decisions that gave the desired outcomes based on successful decisions made in similar circumstances in the past'. Although the analogous examples may be unique and specific to actual critical incidents it might also be the case that the police decision-maker also draws on more archetypal 'schema' (prototypes, scripts, familiar sequences of events with recognisable characters). However, how[34] schema are used in real-life decision-making in critical incident decision-making is unclear. What is true is that we are all willingly employ schema, when, for example, trying

[30] Also called 'modus tollens'.

[31] Some of the most well-known examples of the 'confirmation bias' derive from experiments conducted in the 1960s by Peter Wason, including the 'Wason Card Problem'.

[32] Technically known as the 'premises'.

[33] Often described as the 'reverse' of deduction in the literature although this is somewhat misleading.

[34] Or even if.

Deduction

Induction

may have acted in a certain way. The lim-
)f schemata, suggest that whilst schemata
.uring an investigation, experienced detec-
s in their application. Skilled detectives also
1ese schemata work best with familiar, rou-
lerlying base rates.[35] However, they are far
:vents with low likelihood.[36]
inferences might well be combinations
of these three canonical forms of reasoning, combined in the mind as
complex forms of probabilistic inference.[37] For example, reasoning during a critical incident might be include the use of abduction as an initial 'guess' (or hypothesis, a preliminary 'diagnosis') which is then tested
using deduction (what would logically follow, for example in terms of
the consequences?) and induction (what information/evidence supports or refutes this?). This will lead to an inference being supported,
rejected in favour of alternatives or abandoned altogether. In practice forms of inference are also clustered together and meta inferences
employed to test degrees of coherence; for example, if separate pathways
of abductive reasoning lead us to run with the working hypothesis in
a murder enquiry that 'the offender was left-handed' and 'the offender's blood group was Rhesus negative' then we will naturally attempt to
invoke the form of argument that combines both of these hypothesises
and look within the group of suspects for those individuals with both
characteristics.

CONCLUSIONS

Some circumstances in policing are common, familiar and although
sometimes complicated are not usually unduly complex and remain
largely predictable. Decisions in these settings are likely to be rule-based
('Standard Operating Procedures'), with little need to deviate from
what was learned during training. However, what is perhaps surprising
is that not just many, but probably most decisions in policing demand

---

[35] Such as burglary of domestic properties.

[36] Such as child homicide by stranger with a sexual motive.

[37] The subject of ongoing neurological research.

reasoning in circumstances which are novel (often unique) and unfamiliar. This is particularly the case with the critical incident. Decisions during these incidents often have to be in quick time by exercising swift judgement by choosing between options (including the choice of not to act). Inevitably, complex situations have to be simplified in the human mind with the number of options considered at any one time severely limited. It will not always be possible to apply strictly analytical 'rational' models of decision-making (those that attempt to methodically estimate likelihoods, risks and outcomes) at all points within particular critical incidents that demand forceful action. As Staller and Zaiser (2015, p. 6) caution '[…] decision-making models for police use of force, which are based on traditional decision-making, are too complex to use proficiently once an immediate threat is posed'. As discussed in this chapter, there are also intuitive, frugal and rapid ways of making the right decisions especially when these ways are tempered with learning through experience. Our innate decision-making (such as heuristics) follows the logic of adaptation through natural and other forms of selection and has been highly successful in the past. However, these inherited forms of deciding reflect more the circumstances of our ancestral past rather than the era of suicidal terrorists wielding Kalashnikovs in city centres. The future will probably see more automated forms of reasoning for rapid decision-making in critical incident policing, particularly with the advent of machine learning and improved technical support. In the meantime it is humans either alone, or more often with others, that will undertake most of the reasoning in critical incidents. Perhaps therefore the most important conclusion resides in the importance of police officers' self-awareness of the nature of intuitive and more conscious forms of decision-making used in critical incidents, and a deeper understanding of the strengths and weaknesses of the canonical forms of reasoning employed. This 'reasoning self-awareness' is particularly important in countering the effects of cognitive bias. It echoes Charles Darwin's advice to other naturalists engaged in scientific enquiry to immediately write down any experimental results inconsistent with their hypotheses for he had resolved '… that whenever a published fact, a new observation or thought came across to me, which was opposed to my general results, to make a memorandum of it without fail and at once, for I had found by experience that such facts and thoughts were far more apt to escape from the memory than favourable ones' (Barlow 1958, p. 123 cited in Denzin and Lincoln 2011, p. 309).

REFERENCES

Brighton, H., & Gigerenzer, G. (2012, July–September). Homo Heuristicus: Less-Is-More Effects in Adaptive Cognition. *Malaysian Journal of Medical Sciences, 19*(4), 6–16.

College of Policing. (2015). *Critical Incident Management Introduction and Types of Critical Incidents* [Online]. Available at https://www.app.college.police.uk/app-content/critical-incident-management/types-of-critical-incident/.

Cosmides, L., & Tooby, J. (1992). Cognitive Adaptations for Social Exchange. In J. Barkow, L. Cosmides, & J. Tooby (Eds.), *The Adapted Mind: Evolutionary Psychology and the Generation of Culture*. Oxford: Oxford University Press.

Cosmides, L., Barrett, H., & Tooby, J. (2010). Adaptive Specializations, Social Exchange, and the Evolution of Human Intelligence. In J. Avise & F. Ayala (Eds.), *In the Light of Evolution IV: The Human Condition*. Washington, DC: The National Academies Press.

Denzin, N., & Lincoln, Y. (Eds.). (2011). *The Sage Handbook of Qualitative Research*. London: Sage.

Donoso, M., Collins, A., & Koechlin, E. (2014). Foundations of Human Reasoning in the Prefrontal Cortex. *Science, 344*(6191), 1481–1486.

Eastwood, J., Snook, B., & Luther, K. (2012). What People Want From Their Professionals: Attitudes Toward Decision-Making Strategies. *Journal of Behavioural Decision Making, 25*, 458–468.

Eyre, M., & Alison, L. (2007). To Decide or Not to Decide: Decision Making and Decision Avoidance in Critical Incidents. In D. Carson, B. Milne, F. Pakes, K. Shalev, & A. Shawyer (Eds.), *Applying Psychology to Criminal Justice*. Chichester: Wiley.

Eyre, M., & Alison, L. (2010). Investigative Decision Making. In J. Brown & E. Campbell (Eds.), *The Cambridge Handbook of Forensic Psychology*. Cambridge: Cambridge University Press.

Findley, K., & Scott, M. (2006). The Multiple Dimensions of Tunnel Vision in Criminal Cases. *Wisconsin Law Review* [Online]. Available at https://media.law.wisc.edu/m/hyjb3/findley_scott_final.pdf.

Garrett, M. (2014). Complexity of Our Brain. *Psychology Today* [Online]. Available at https://www.psychologytoday.com/blog/iage/201402/complexity-our-brain.

Gilovich, T., Griffin, D., & Kahneman, D. (Eds.). (2002). *Heuristics and Biases: The Psychology of Intuitive Judgment*. Cambridge: Cambridge University Press.

Hammerstein, P., & Stevens, J. (2012). *Six Reasons for Invoking Evolution in Decision Theory in Evolution and the Mechanisms of Decision Making* (Ernst Strüngmann Forum Report, Vol. 11, pp. 1–17). Cambridge, MA: MIT Press.

Hoffrage, U., & Gigerenzer, G. (1998). Using Natural Frequencies to Improve Diagnostic Reasoning. *Academic Medicine, 73,* 538–540.

Hoffrage, U., Krauss, S., Martignon, L., & Gigerenzer, G. (2015, October). Natural Frequencies Improve Bayesian Reasoning in Simple and Complex Inference Tasks. *Frontiers in Psychology, 6,* Article 1473.

Johnson, D., Blumstein, D., Fowler, J., & Haselton, M. (2013, August). The Evolution of Error: Error Management, Cognitive Constraints, and Adaptive Decision-Making Biases. *Trends in Ecology & Evolution, 28*(8), 474–481.

Kahneman, D., & Tversky, A. (Eds.). (2000). *Choices, Values and Frames.* Cambridge: Cambridge University Press.

Kenrick, D., Norman, P., & Butner, J. (2003). Dynamical Evolutionary Psychology: Individual Decision Rules and Emergent Social Norms. *Psychological Review, 110*(1), 3–28.

Koehler, D. & Harvey, N. (Eds.). (2004). *Blackwell Handbook of Judgment & Decision Making.* Oxford: Blackwell.

Lipshitz, R., & Ben Shaul, O. (1997). Schemata and Mental Models in Recognition-Primed Decision Making. In C. Zsambok & G. Klein (Eds.), *Naturalistic Decision Making.* Mahwah, NJ: Lawrence Erlbaum Associates.

Lipton, P. (1991). *Inference to the Best Explanation.* London: Routledge.

Magnani, L. (2001). *Abduction, Reason, and Science.* Dordrecht: Kluwer.

Mata, R., Pachur, T., von Helversen, B., Rieskamp, J., & Schooler, L. (2012). Ecological Rationality: A Framework for Understanding and Aiding the Aging Decision Maker. *Frontiers in Neuroscience, 6,* 19.

Meder, B., & Gigerenzer, G. (2014). Statistical Thinking: No One Left Behind. In E. Chernoff & B. Sriraman (Eds.), *Probabilistic Thinking, Advances in Mathematics Education.* Dordrecht: Springer Science & Business Media.

Mellers, B. (1996, March). From the President Society for Judgment and Decision Making. *Newsletter, XV*(1) [Online]. Available at http://www.sjdm.org/newsletters/96-mar.html#2.

Mousavi, S., & Gigerenzer, G. (2014, August). Risk, Uncertainty, and Heuristics. *Journal of Business Research, 67*(8), 1671–1678.

Orquin, J. L., & Kurzban, R. (2016). A Meta-analysis of Blood Glucose Effects on Human Decision Making. *Psychological Bulletin, 142*(5), 546–567.

Patokorpi, E. (2007). Logic of Sherlock Holmes in Technology Enhanced Learning. *Educational Technology & Society, 10*(1), 171–185.

Pease, K., & Roach, J. (2017). How to Morph Experience into Evidence. In J. Knuttson & L. Tompson (Eds.), *Advances in Evidence Based Policing* (pp. 84–97). London: Routledge (ISBN 978-1-138 69873).

Pinker, S. (2003). *How the Mind Works.* London: Penguin Books.

Roach, J., & Pease, K. (2013). *Evolution and Crime.* London: Routledge.

Salet, R., & Terpstra, J. (2013). Critical Review in Criminal Investigation: Evaluation of a Measure to Prevent Tunnel Vision. *Policing, 8*(1), 43–50.

Schum D., & Starace, S. (1994). *The Evidential Foundations of Probabilistic Reasoning*. Chichester: Wiley.

Schurz, G. (2008). Patterns of Abduction. *Syntheses, 164*, 201–234.

Sharps, M. (2010). *Processing Under Pressure: Stress, Memory and Decision-Making in Law Enforcement*. Flushing, NY: Looseleaf Law Publications.

Snook, B., & Cullen, R. (2009). Bounded Rationality and Criminal Investigations: Has Tunnel Vision Been Wrongfully Convicted? In K. Rossmo (Ed.), *Criminal Investigative Failures*. London: CRC Press.

Staller, M., & Zaiser, B. (2015). Developing Problem Solvers: New Perspectives on Pedagogical Practices in Police Use of Force Training. *Journal of Law Enforcement, 4*(3).

Starckea, K., & Branda, M. (2012, April). Decision Making Under Stress: A Selective Review. *Neuroscience & Biobehavioral Reviews, 36*(4), 1228–1248.

Todd, P., & Gigerenzer, G. (1999). *Simple Heuristics That Make Us Smart* [Online]. Available at http://www-abc.mpib-berlin.mpg.de/users/ptodd/SimpleHeuristics.BBS/.

CHAPTER 5

How a Major Incident Room Operates and the Management of Critical Incidents Ex DCI Harland N Yorks Police

Adam Harland

Abstract Harland states that the investigation of homicide can be broken down into the search for the suspect(s) and the building of a case against them. He concentrates on the mechanics of the Major Incident Room, the MIR. This is the formal organization of a major police enquiry incorporating the 'HOLMES' database, which has a number of weaknesses including "timeliness" which is a handicap in the initial stages of an investigation. A second challenge is the sequencing of events. Time and place are central elements of the SIO's initial parameters and are often the basis of eliminations from enquiries where there is no direct physical evidence as elimination criteria. The role of the SIO has become increasingly managerial, reliant on the synthesis of material by others rather than their own direct judgement of that material.

A. Harland (✉)
University of Exeter, Exeter, UK
e-mail: adam.harland@north.yorkshire.ac.uk

© The Author(s) 2019
M. Roycroft and J. Roach (eds.),
Decision Making in Police Enquiries and Critical Incidents,
https://doi.org/10.1057/978-1-349-95847-4_5

Keywords Major Incident Room · Home Office Large Major Enquiry
System (HOLMES) · Byford report · Managerial

> Realising the importance of the case, my men are rounding up twice the
> usual number of suspects

With this explanation Captain Renault, the morally compromised Chief
of Police and symbol of Vichy France in the 1942 film Casablanca, seeks
to assure his German superior, Major Strasser, that he is investigating
diligently. Claude Rains' character may well have been given some of
the best comic lines by the scriptwriters but he also accurately reflects
the sometimes desperate hopes of many a senior investigator; that more
activity will, or will be believed to produce better results.

This chapter looks at the competing responses to the demands of
activity and analysis within the investigation of a critical incident. Central
to the balancing of this juxtaposition will be a consideration of the operation of the MIR (Major Incident Room) and the roles and technologies
that are employed in analysing the product of investigative activity, and
identifying fruitful activity from that analysis.

The standard policing definition of a critical incident is 'any incident
where the effectiveness of the police response is likely to have a significant impact on the confidence of the victim, their family and/or the
community'.[1] Such incidents are far from restricted to homicide enquiries, but such enquiries are a core function of the state's assurance of
the Article 2 Right to Life. In this context, a 'successful' investigation
is the proper identification of the agent(s) of a homicide, sufficient for
the legal system to assure the wider community that the risk of subsequent harm from this source is adequately managed. Few headlines can
be envisaged as impacting on public confidence in the Police with the
force of 'Killer strikes again!'.

The management of homicide investigations has been the subject of
much comment and some study. The study has tended to identify two
areas of consistency.

---

[1] College of Policing (2013): *Introduction and Types of Critical Incidents* [Internet].
https://www.app.college.police.uk/app-content/critical-incident-management/
types-of-critical-incident/ (Accessed 26 January 2016).

The first is that homicide has a high and reasonably consistent 'clear up' rate. In 2004 Home Office research identified that the 90% clear up rate 'is often used as an indicator of investigative performance, in an effort to justify and legitimate the police's investigative methodologies for this aspect of their work'[2]. The Office of National Statistics Homicide figures for 2014 suggest that no suspect has been charged in relation to offences in 2012/2013 in 16% of cases, noting that continued investigations would bring further suspects within this figure. The similar figure for the two previous years showed 12 and 9% of cases without suspects, supporting the assertion that continued enquiries resulted in subsequent suspect identification.

Both sources also point out that a police 'clear up' is not the same as a successful prosecution, with a quarter of all homicide cases between 1989 and 1999 resulting in the acquittal of all parties.[3]

The other consistency is the role of swift action upon the discovery of the homicide. Thus there are 'golden' hours[4] which are, correctly, seen as of central importance in preserving, and subsequently exploiting, evidence. This is particularly of importance for the recovery of contact trace material, a potent source for the cellular biometrics that has created the 'DNA' revolution in UK homicide enquiries in the last 25 years.[5]

Significant resources are allocated to the control of 'scenes' and the associated examinations, with consequent evidential knowledge.

The investigation of homicide can be broken down into the 'Who done it' and the 'Why done it' types of investigation, being in direct terms the search for the suspect(s) and the building of a case against them. What have been described as the 'self solvers'[6] reflect the personal nature of homicide. Many homicides arise from factors closely related to the personal life of the victim, which creates circumstances where the identification of the suspect is swift, and the focus of the investigation can be directed

[2] Home Office Homicide review 25/04, p. 11.

[3] 25/04.

[4] College of Policing (2013): *Investigation Process* [Internet]. https://www.app.college. police.uk/app-content/investigations/investigation-process/ (Accessed 26 January 2016), see in particular Para 7.4.2 within this module.

[5] The first conviction for murder based upon what was then called 'DNA fingerprint' was of Colin Pitchfork in 1988.

[6] Innes M., both in 'The Process Structures of Police Homicide Investigations,' *British Journal of Criminology* 42 (2002), 669–688 and in *Investigating Murder: Detective Work and the Police Response to Criminal Homicide*. Oxford: Clarendon Press, 2003.

at the collation of evidence to satisfy the requirements of proof of legal intent. While these enquiries may be wide ranging, they are predominantly straightforward, and in the latter stages of the legal process informed by the requirements of the prosecuting authority and presenting counsel.

The most recent analysis of the relationship between victim and offender shows that the immediate personal life of the victim is closely linked to suspect identification. 45% of female homicide victims are killed by partners or ex-partners, with other family members taking the total to 68%. Domestic violence is less deadly for male victims, but it is friends or associates who are identified as suspects in 35% of these deaths. In total, female victims know the suspect, in some manner in 79% of cases, with male victims having a direct association with their killer in 45% of cases.[7] These levels of association between victim and suspect greatly assist in providing 'self solvers', offering a rapid movement from the 'who done it' to 'why done it' investigative priority. In these cases it would appear that Captain Renault's 'usual suspects' is an approach that has a degree of statistical validity.

Recent changes in policing policies towards domestic violence are a matter of current commentary in relation to the reduction in the numbers of homicide.[8] Active prevention strategies are not, however, an investigative tool, so that where a suspect is not swiftly identified, a homicide investigation is likely to become the concern of a MIR.

In discussion here, the MIR is the formal organisation of a major police enquiry with, specifically, the use of information technology to assist the enquiry. In most cases this will refer to the 'HOLMES' arrangements.[9] This itself has seen two major operating incarnations and a series of version updates, and has been the agreed national policing system for over 20 years. The standardised operating procedures are outlined in the 280 page MIRSAP manual,[10] providing a template for the linking and interchange between enquiries nationwide.

[7] Office of National Statistics, Focus on Violent Crime and Sexual Offences, Chapter 2 Homicide 2012/3 Published February 2014.

[8] The homicide rate for the year ending March 2017 was still 20% lower than 10 years ago (13.2 homicides per million population compared with 10.5 homicides per million population—excluding Hillsborough). http://www.ons.gov.uk.

[9] 'Home Office Large & Major Enquiry System'. First introduced in 1986, with an agreement to move to HOLMES 2 in 1994. The current system is provided under a PFI agreement with Unisys.

[10] Major Incident Room Standardised Administrative Procedures (MIRSAP) 2005 ©ACPO is the current guidance.

The immediate driver for the adoption of such a system came from the Byford report into the Yorkshire Ripper.[11] Using an index card carousel system to log and collate information, the 'incident room became overwhelmed by a welter of information'. Although not the only area to be criticised, the administration of the collation of evidence was a central failing, delaying the identification of Peter Sutcliffe as the offender.

Byford saw this administrative confusion as having a *"direct effect of frustrating the work of SIOs and junior detectives alike"*, and pointed to technology and standardisation of procedures as offering a solution.[12]

There are, however a number of weaknesses of the HOLMES system. The Murder Investigation Manual states that the SIO must be in charge of the MIR, and not the other way around, which suggests that this is not always the case, and anecdotal comment is often made around the frustrations of HOLMES 'running' the enquiry.

The first weakness is a matter of timeliness. This is a considerable handicap in the initial stages of an investigation, where significant areas of knowledge are lacking and the decision making is based upon limited and sometimes inaccurate information.[13] The conflicting demands of control and activity within this period is highlighted within the Murder Investigation Manual with the first two of the three paragraphs within this section starting with the phrase 'Experienced SIOs',[14] emphasising the subjective basis of the earliest decision making within a homicide enquiry. What is quite clear is that the SIO, experienced or otherwise, will have enough to consider without an immediate concentration on administrative arrangements.

Elsewhere 'experienced' may be seen as those best equipped to deal with the demands of 'situational awareness'.[15] This is most pithily

---

[11] A summary of the report by HMCIC Byford was published in 1981, with the fuller details released in 2006, following a Freedom of Information Act submission.

[12] For a review of recurring themes within challenged Major enquiries, See Roycroft M., 'Historical Analysis of Public Inquiries of Homicide Investigations,' *The Journal of Homicide and Major Incident Investigation* 4 (2, Autumn), (2008), 43–58.

[13] Para 2.2.5 The 'Golden Hour' Principle. Murder Investigation Manual regarding the balances required of an 'experienced SIO', p. 42.

[14] The phrase 'Experienced SIO' is used only 5 times in total within the 301 page document, and nowhere else within the manual during a discussion of the activity of the SIO.

[15] Variously described in Cook T and Tattersall SIO Handbook, Balckstones 2014 Sec 2.3, p. 30 and in ACPO Practice Advice on Core Investigative Doctrine, NPIA 2012 p. 88.

described as 'knowing what is going on around you'[16] or the 'accessibility of a comprehensive and coherent situational representation which is continually being updated in accordance with the results of recurrent situation assessments'.[17]

Even with the adoption of pre-prepared action lists, the processing of information within the HOLMES arrangements takes time and a number of staff to produce a flow of consequential actions. The HOLMES system is envisaged as an information registration, indexing and collation process, creating an auditable trail for how and why each piece of information is within the enquiry. In the early stages of a homicide investigation, these are not primary functions, and many organisations prefer to utilise a proprietary task management system to record and control who is doing what and then recording if it has been done.[18] The auditable features of electronic records provide a preferable solution to the previous practice of 'paper actions' with the perennial problems of lost paperwork and incomplete activity logs. As will be discussed below, however, the investigative methodology underpinning HOLMES relates to early and accurate identification of parameters by the SIO in order to work most efficiently.

The subsequent disadvantage of the under pinning methodology of the HOLMES system is what now may be referred as the Rumsfeld conundrum of the 'unknown unknowns'.[19] The impacts of this are best understood from an examination of how the system is designed to work.

Whether by chance or design, HOLMES is a reductive investigative methodology, reflecting the words of the great, but fictional, detective himself; "Once you eliminate the impossible, whatever remains, no matter how improbable, must be the truth".[20] In the most simplified of expressions, this relies upon the coincidence of the suspect and the victim at a time and place. The SIO has to determine the relevant time and place, identify all the persons who were present within those times,

---

[16] SIO handbook, as above.

[17] ACPO Core Practice as above, citing the *International Journal of Aviation Psychology* 1, 45–57.

[18] The task management system provided by Clio Software is widely adopted for this purpose.

[19] Popularly attributed to Donald Rumsfeld in a US Department of Defence briefing given on 12 February 2002, although alternately cited from elsewhere.

[20] Doyle C. *The Sign of the Four*. 1890 Chapter 6.

and then eliminate them as a suspect until, at least theoretically, whoever is not eliminated is the offender. The setting of the initial parameters is therefore an immediate limiting factor to the scope of the enquiry.

The process of the HOLMES system is that information[21] arrives with the Receiver, who may identify the need for an immediate enquiry (an 'action') before allowing the information into the system by passing it to an Indexer for registration. The registered information is passed to the Document Reader. The role of this position is central to the functioning of the process. The Document Reader 'marks up' the information which creates two main types of activity; indexing and actions. Indexing is the process of recording specific information, which includes the process of creating a 'nominal', which is the record of a person within the enquiry. The person does not have to be identified to be a record, indeed in the initial stages of an enquiry; much of the investigative effort is directed at identifying these unknown nominals. Each nominal will be created only as a result of appearing in some information, and further text indexing and linking will record any further known details. The raising of an action is the identification of a line of enquiry arising from the information. This 'mark up' will be within parameters set by the SIO, as to relevance and urgency (priority).

The identified indexing and actions are passed to an Indexer, who creates the records required. The actions raised are passed to the Action Allocator who manages the distribution of the enquiries within the available investigative staff. This, again, is in response to the priorities required by the SIO.

The actions that are allocated produce more information, and this recreates the cycle above. Each new piece of information has the potential to generate further activity, but not necessarily information relevant to the process of elimination. If the suspect has been successfully identified, the accumulation of evidence is a necessary step towards assisting a correct interpretation of the intention of the offender, but where the offender is not yet identified, the investigative focus should be on determining who did commit the offence.

The HOLMES system creates 'a comprehensive and coherent situational representation', but it does not do so quickly, and is resource intensive. Where the division of roles is intended to allow for the

---

[21] Information is used here as a generic description for the range of Statement, Officer's reports, Messages and other means by which information is delivered to the MIR.

checking of information[22] and activity, the response to limited resources through role sharing (or 'double hatting') has created criticism of both the enquiry and of senior police management.[23]

A second challenge of the management of enquiries that constitute a critical incident also relates to time, not as initially in regard to timeliness but as to sequencing of events. The sequence of events is, self-evidently, a critical tool in understanding the relationship of cause and effect contained within the evidence gathered. This is more than just the intellectual construct of a 'story' that helps the understanding of investigators, prosecutors and those presenting the evidence to a jury. Time and place are central elements of the SIO's initial parameters and are often the basis of eliminations from enquiries where there is no direct physical evidence as elimination criteria.

The use of this synthesis of the evidence may be used several times in the course of any enquiry, with initial interest in the events relating to the victim, and subsequent concentration relating to the events associated with the offender, often as an aid to motive.

Initial versions of HOLMES provided a facility to create a Sequence of Events (SOE) which provided a partially successful response to this need, but in a form that was difficult to read as an integrated summary. The complexity of interpretation was weighed against the significant indexing time that was required and usage diminished, not least during the period of significant advances in the contribution of forensic science from the mid-1990s onwards.

The move from the use of indexing within HOLMES to the use of analysts and analytical tools was in place, and was identified as good practice, by the Soham enquiry.[24] This has created a further demand for specialist skills, which the SIO will have to address from a position of lack of knowledge and limited resources. Would the best decision be to concentrate analytical resources on the insights provided by a SOE or on the inter-relationships revealed by mobile communications, in an ever-expanding arena of devices and potential evidence sources? Delaying resource deployment from one area will result in a consequent delay for

[22] See below for further discussion of the 'abc' of investigation.

[23] See in particular the MacPherson report S16.11 and all of Sec 20.

[24] See the Flanaghan Report on the Soham Murders 5.72 Time Line document … ran to 99 pages. It was subsequently described by the principal CPS lawyer as '*the single most useful document that came out of operation Fincham*'.

'catch-up', during which a 'critical' enquiry may be active but without the intellectual stimulus to understanding that a new analysis of the evidence brings.

This is also an area that highlights the increasing dependence of the SIO of information provided by the interpretation of a single individual, with specialist skills.

Reading the Byford report illustrates the increase in the role of specialist knowledge, and the widening SIO responsibilities over some 30 years; biological science and mobile telephony require explanation by intermediaries, as the base material is incomprehensible to the non-expert, even at the most basic level. Family Liaison and Community Impact responsibilities expand exponentially as an enquiry becomes a 'critical' incident. Human Rights, and consequent, legislation requires a deeper involvement in the management of searches, the use of legal powers, judicial applications and the full range of covert policing techniques. Twenty-four hour and social media create demand and opportunities which have to be managed, with image capture by the public presenting further opportunities to CCTV coverage as an evidence source. The demands of internal strategies to be agreed are numerous.

None of these areas are unimportant or without consequence to the overall enquiry, but are in addition to the basic process of investigation. The 'flattening of the pyramid' of command within forces means that most homicide team SIOs are DCI, reporting to D/Supt ranks. In the case of 'critical incident' enquiries the deployment of the D/Supt is a likely response, resulting in an SIO with further management responsibilities outside the immediate enquiry.

It is the role of the SIO to balance these demands and arrange the evidence sources into a coherent explanation of events. The range of demands limits the amount of time that can be spent in any one area, reducing the ability of the SIO to apply the basic 'abc' of investigation (Accept nothing, Believe no one, Check everything)[25] in an environment where specialism produces a single source which perforce will be accepted and believed and which is difficult to check.

The structure within the HOLMES system is intended to do such checking, by recording and indexing to identify gaps in knowledge or evidential conflicts for further investigation. This is achieved in regard to

[25] See examples at SIO Handbook Sec 2.5 'ABC Rule' p. 31, or ACPO Core Investigative Doctrine p. 88.

word-based records of statements, interviews and officers' reports, but is less successful with image, physical or database evidence. The abundance of material can easily overwhelm the ability to index and without this the system is reduced in its effectiveness as an investigative tool.

SMART searching provides certain advantages in rapid identification of potentially relevant material, but brings with it quality control issues (especially in self typed reports and statements), and the 'Google' phenomenon, where the first apparently credible response identified amongst multiple responses is the most readily accepted, and further scrutiny deferred.

These factors influence the responses to research into hard to solve cases, where information management is identified as a major contributor to the lack of success.[26] Increased information management technology was successfully applied to homicide investigation following the Byford report, but increasingly the broadening scale of potential evidence sources is creating a situation where information management fails and overwhelms an enquiry.

The role of the SIO has become increasingly managerial, reliant on the synthesis of material by others rather than their own direct judgement of that material. There are many advantages to a broad and varied consideration of evidential material, but with a collegiate approach to evidence presentation also comes the risk of unclear lines of decision making. It is inevitable that specialist knowledge creates a belief in the viability of specific techniques in providing a resolution to the enquiry, with experiential knowledge of previous 'successes' for this technique highlighted. The SIO themselves will bring a body of experience based upon their previous involvement in enquiries, with a hierarchy of previously successful techniques.

To this is added the imposition of the Gold Command[27] structure in response to a critical incident. This is a clear and sensible response to the wider impacts of the enquiry, which fall outside the expertise of the SIO and involve resources beyond their control. The difficulty lies with the mixed role of the SIO as 'silver', falling between a strategic role for the conduct of the enquiry and subordination to the wider Gold strategy.

This is another diversion for the SIO from the direction of the enquiry and provides another demand upon the incident room for the provision

---

[26] See Roycroft as above, and Home Office Homicide Review 25/04.
[27] See ACPO Guidance on Command and Control 2009.

of management information to inform the Gold Command deliberations, as well as pressures to challenge the policy of the SIO. It can lead to the situation where it is not clear who is in command.[28]

The impact of confusion of command is, amongst other effects, that there is a falling back upon method, both as a defensive mechanism by the SIO and as a support for a lack of experience. In particular the desire to be involved in positive action can influence an over reliance on the process of TIE[29] identification in circumstances where there is insufficient evidence to allow for effective elimination. The population of a list is a relatively easy task, especially in a case of a female victim where Registered Sex Offenders are an apparently directly relevant category.

It has previously been illustrated that the threats to female homicide victims reside strongly within their family and friendship groups. It is also the case that most sexual offenders are manipulative of relationships in their offending and only a small proportion act in a predatory manner towards strangers. Research into the criminal careers of such offenders suggests that is uncertain how to prioritise risk. The aim of the process of investigation is based on reducing the list of potential suspects, not on creating or expanding it.

The successful application of biometric material, in particular in homicide enquiries, has diluted the understanding of the basic activity of investigation system, which is reductive. A DNA 'hit' has become evidence of involvement, whereas in detail it is the evidence that the probability of there being another provider of this DNA profile is small enough to be presented as 'beyond reasonable doubt'. This is reflected in the advice of the prosecuting authority seeking for 'some other supporting evidence' beyond the DNA evidence.[30] Where the benefits of DNA identification

---

[28] Flanaghan Report, see especially Recommendation 2, referencing Sec 5.49 'Ironically, the overlaying of the Gold, Silver, Bronze command structure on this operation contributed to a lack of clarity of command of the incident, particularly in relation to the role of the SIO'.

[29] Variously interpreted as 'Trace Interview and Eliminate' or 'Trace, Implicate or Eliminate'.

[30] CPS Guidance on DNA Charging, Including National Tripartite Protocol, Local FSP Protocol templates, Staged Reporting procedure, new MGFSP form, 2004.

5.4 In the light of this, a suspect should not be charged solely on the basis of a match between his DNA profile and a DNA profile found at the scene of the crime, unless there are compelling reasons to do so. It is imperative that under the change in policy, the speculative DNA evidence will need to be evaluated with at least some other supporting evidence in the case.

lie is in the early concentration of investigative efforts on a determined direction, allowing for evidence identification and recovery in a period before records are destroyed and memories become unreliable.

The most significant source of evidence to identify the offender comes from the crime scene, the most important element of which is the body of the victim. Without a body, a potential identification of the offender is weakened, as only where and not who can be unhesitatingly asserted. Without a scene the challenges increase exponentially.

These are exactly the factors that have determined the priority given to the golden 'hour'. As evidence degrades and disappears through the various timescales of biology, overwritten CCTV and the working of the human memory, the prospects for an early identification of 'who done it', releasing the detailed work of 'what/why done it' becomes ever smaller. In achieving this, DNA identification has shown itself to be the elimination tool par excellence.

The swift notification of finding a body, or noticing a person is missing, allows for rapid responses and 'golden' activity. With an increasing pattern of independent single householders,[31] there will remain a number of investigations where the need for action was not identified soon enough for the benefits of this activity. If there is no DNA shortcut to suspect identification then the SIO is faced by mounting challenges. The lack of swift identification will increase the social pressure leading to a 'critical incident'. This will bring with it demands from a 'Gold' structure, which will require application to be diverted away from the management of the core investigative process. The initial identification of parameters, so heavily associated within the Murder Investigation Manual with experience, will become the determinant of the success of the process of elimination. What is the evidence that will allow for elimination from suspicion and which resources should seek these determinant factors. All the while the HOLMES system, awash with people who may have done it, will be producing activity to be undertaken. The volume of information will increase, and the reliance on the individual skills of SPOCs become unavoidable.

---

[31]See Office of National Statistics I MacRory @measuring National Well Being—Households and Families 2012. 29% of households are one person, representing 7.7 million people. Isolation, or familial/relationship threats diminish the likelihood or early notification or discovery of a missing person in these circumstances.

In the face of all these pressures, the SIO may wish to recall that Captain Renault had no intention of capturing his offenders. Activity in an investigation is not always investigative activity. The correct emphasis on the recovery of evidence in the golden hours is the first part of a successful investigation. The role of the SIO is to understand how to objectively and ethically reduce the plethora of information. It is part of the process of, but not the aim of the investigation to identify who may have committed the offence. In the face of the increasing pressure inherent in a critical incident the SIO is assisted in understanding the basis of the processes employed and seek the evidence that allows for the reduction of these usual suspects, or even twice their number, to allow for the concentration of investigative effort on correctly identifying the suspect.

CHAPTER 6

'The Making of an Expert Detective'— A European Perspective: Comparing Decision-Making in Norway and UK

Ivar Fahsing

Abstract Fahsing states that the SIO's decision style and mindset was one of the major "solving factors" in a successful investigation. He discusses the need for increased awareness and strong system-support when moving from suspect identification to verification. His groundbreaking studies of British and Norwegian detectives compared the awareness and quality of investigative decisions made by experienced detectives and novice police officers in two countries with markedly different models for the development of investigative expertise (England and Norway). While the knowledge and awareness of critical factors were remarkably high and consistent in both countries (Study I), did accredited homicide detectives in England vastly outperform novice police officers in the number of reported adequate investigative hypotheses and actions. In Norway however, bachelor educated novices did better than highly experienced homicide detectives. The main factor behind these remarkable findings seems to be differences in national policy, such as professional accreditation and

I. Fahsing (✉)
Norwegian Police University College, Oslo, Norway

© The Author(s) 2019   83
M. Roycroft and J. Roach (eds.),
Decision Making in Police Enquiries and Critical Incidents,
https://doi.org/10.1057/978-1-349-95847-4_6

system support between the two countries. How to best compare and develop detective expertise that might act as a generic safeguard towards such biased decisions has not systematically addressed before.

Keywords Investigative management · Decision-making · Measuring investigative quality · Hypotheses driven investigation · Verification and falsification

The success of criminal investigations depends to a great extent on investigators' ability to make the correct decisions at the correct time. Unfortunately, investigators face a number of obstacles to optimal decision-making, including time pressure, emotional involvement and expediency-promoting occupational norms, all of which have been shown to debilitate investigators' ability to objectively process case-relevant information and evidence (Ask and Granhag 2007a, b; Ask et al. 2011). A particular challenge, amplified by the aforementioned factors, is to resist going from the process of 'suspect identification' to 'verification' at an early stage of the investigation (Stelfox and Pease 2005). That is, although an investigation with potential for prosecution must at some point start building a case against the suspected offender, doing so prematurely may be extremely harmful as evidenced by numerous miscarriages of justice (Findley and Scott 2006). The transition from identification to verification is accompanied by a corresponding shift in detectives' mindset. This notion rests on the theoretical and empirical work by Gollwitzer and colleagues on the different phases of goal-directed behaviour (e.g. Gollwitzer 1990; Gollwitzer et al. 1990). Typically, people tend to be more creative and open-minded before having chosen a specific course of action (i.e. when in a 'deliberative' mindset) and significantly less so once a choice has been made (i.e. when in an 'implemental' mindset; Gollwitzer et al. 1990). Given the necessity of creativity and open-mindedness for successful criminal investigation, it is important to identify 'tipping points' that may trigger such shifts in investigators' mindset and ultimately to develop safeguards against premature shifts. As a first step towards this aim, the present research surveys expert detectives' views of critical tipping points in real-life investigations. Moreover, by comparing the views of highly experienced homicide detectives in Norway and the UK, we provide an indication of the consensus within the expert population independent of any particular legislative system. Although research on detectives' decision-making is still relatively scarce, serious investigative failures may have been avoided if the available knowledge had been applied in a more systematic way (Ask and Alison 2010; Jones et al. 2008; Rossmo 2014; Stelfox and Pease 2005; Westera et al. 2014). So far, only very few countries have acknowledged the need for a policy enforcing the development of systemic countermeasures against investigative errors on the individual and the organisational level (McGrory and Treacy 2012). The vast majority of the European police forces still rely on traditional systems based on the notion of the omnipotent police generalist, as opposed to highly specialised expert detectives. After a number of public scandals, royal commissions and reforms in England and Wales (see e.g., Tong 2009; O'Neill 2018; Ask and Fahsing 2018), all investigations that are defined as major crime enquiries are subject to the requirement of documenting decision logs, policy files, and written reviews (ACPO 2005; 2007; 2010). These routines were all part of the national guideline called the Murder Investigation Manual (ACPO 2000; 2006). Additionally, there has been a drive to improve the competence of all police officers and staff tasked with conducting investigations through the introduction of the Professionalizing Investigation Program (James and Mills 2012; McGrory and Treacy 2012). Moreover, full-scale exercises in so-called Hydra decision-making simulation suites are compulsory to all PIP levels, both operative and strategic. Hydra is a high-fidelity immersive simulation training system designed to facilitate the development of operational decision-making skills, cooperation, and review (Eyre et al. 2008). It can be specifically tailored to develop the strategic and critical decision making skills of Senior Investigating Officers (Alison and Crego 2008). Although some of these initiatives and programmes have been criticised and even terminated (see e.g., James and Mills 2012; Hallenberg et al. 2016; Ask and Fahsing 2018), very few countries have developed and implemented anything close to this. This fact motivates comparative studies of detectives operating under different policy regimes.

Norway/European

Despite a number of high profile cases of serious miscarriage of justice in Scandinavia and Europe (Fahsing and Rachlew 2009; Persak 2014; Rachlew 2009) no comparable change of policy towards standardised investigative methods, operational procedures and detectives' professional roles has yet been taken in Norway or any other Scandinavian country (Fahsing 2013; Hald 2011; Rachlew 2009; Riksadvokaten 2015). Although the Norwegian Police University College offers a wide range of different further education programmes within criminal investigation, none of these are compulsory to become a full-time detective (Politidirektoratet 2013). Thus, the traditional belief in an omnipotent police officer still seems to be alive in Norway and most other European countries (Dale 1994; Fahsing 2013). Furthermore, there are no standardised procedures to ensure documentation of investigation plans, critical decisions or systematic quality reviews (Politidirektoratet 2013; Riksadvokaten 2015). On the other hand, all Norwegian police officers must undertake a three-year full-time bachelor in policing before they can apply for a position in the service. This system speaks for a robust police generalist, who is expected to engage in complex tasks without further formal specialisation. From the above, it is evident that the paths to detective expertise are quite different in the two jurisdictions.

The results of the present research indicate that detective-expertise might act as an effective safeguard towards biased decision-makings if developed under the right conditions. Hence, lengthy experience alone does not predict sound judgments, nor decisions, in critical stages of criminal investigations, whereas higher education might represent a solid foundation for the making of an expert detective. The research was split into 2 studies; Study I—an interview study—explored criminal detectives' views of critical factors related to decision-making in homicide investigations. The aim of Study II was to test and compare police officers' ability to make high-quality investigative decisions and to resist the influence of decisional tipping-points.

In Study I, experienced homicide investigators in Norway ($n = 15$) and the UK ($n = 20$) were asked to identify decisional 'tipping-points'—decisions that changed the detectives mindset from being focused on suspect identification to verifying the guilt of a suspect—and situational or individual factors which relate to these decisions. In a content analysis were two types of decision identified as typical and potentially critical tipping points: (1) decisions to point-out, arrest, or charge a suspect and (2) decisions on main strategies and lines of inquiry in the case. Moreover, 10 individual factors (e.g. experience) and 14 situational factors (e.g. information availability) were reported as related to the likelihood of mindset shifts, most of which correspond well with findings in previous decision-making research. The consensus between British and Norwegian detectives was very high, and the findings indicate that experienced detectives are aware of many of the risk factors and obstacles to optimal decision-making that exist in criminal investigations. Study II, using a quasi-experimental design, compared the quality of investigative decisions made by experienced detectives and novice police officers in two countries with markedly different models for the development of investigative expertise (England and Norway). In England, accredited homicide detectives vastly outperformed novice police officers in the number of reported adequate investigative hypotheses and actions. In Norway, however, bachelor educated police novices did marginally better than highly experienced homicide detectives. Taken together, the research in this thesis suggests that investigative judgments are highly susceptible to situational and individual differences.

Critical decisions: Only two types of decisions were identified by the participants as typical and potentially critical tipping points. The decision to name, arrest, or charge a suspect was mentioned by all of the participants (e.g. 'The decision to make an arrest ties you up both mentally and resource-wise', 'All steps towards suspect identification and apprehension—especially at an early stage'). The second type of decisions concerned the choice of main strategies and connected lines of inquiry in the case and was mentioned by 63% of participants (e.g. 'What strategies you decide to set out and follow in your evidence gathering is crucial', 'The lines of inquiry you choose to follow at the outset are of course extremely important'). As can be seen in Table 6.1, the consensus between British and Norwegian detectives was high.

Situational factors: Situational influences on investigators' decision-making were the most frequently reported group of factors. Because of the large number of categories, they were collapsed into four superordinate categories, representing major themes. The four themes were, in order of frequency (Table 6.1):

1. availability of information/
2. evidence (e.g. 'Information is the lifeblood of any investigation'), 'Strong evidence available at outset is normally a good thing—but it can also be fatal if not challenged correctly'),
3. external pressure/community impact (e.g. Nowadays, mass media is there with an enormous impact already from the first

Table 6.1 Tipping-points in frequency of mentioned in interviews ($N = 35$)

	Norwegian (n=15)	British (n=20)
	Critical Decisions (CD)	
To name, arrest and to charge a suspect	15 (100%)	20 (100%)
Hypothesis, lines of inquiry and main strategies	9 (60%)	13 (65%)
	Situational factors impacting on CD	
Availability of information and potential evidence	15 (100%)	20 (100%)
Strong and potentially stereotypical evidence	10 (70%)	14 (67%)
Pressures from outside and community-impact	15 (100%)	20 (100%)
Who is involved?	15 (100%)	19 (95%)
High media attention	15 (100%)	18 (90%)
Nature of the case	12 (80%)	18 (92%)
Political issues involved	12 (80%)	15 (73%)
Role of the defence lawyer	8 (53%)	1 (5%)
Pressures from inside and organizational issues	15 (100%)	20 (100%)
Availability of resources main	15 (100%)	18 (90%)
– Skilled personnel	15 (100%)	17 (85%)
– Finances	13 (87%)	13 (65%)
– Technology	12 (80%)	10 (50%)
– Workload	12 (80%)	10 (45%)
Management and team culture	13 (87%)	16 (80%)
Systems and organizational knowledge	11 (73%)	14 (70%)
Force-reputation	8 (54%)	13 (65%)
Preceding decisions made in the case	9 (57%)	8 (40%)
Review and revisions	3 (20%)	12 (60%)
Time-pressure	13 (86%)	14 (70%)
	Individual factors impacting on CD	
Detective experience and field knowledge	15 (100%)	20 (100%)
Relevant training and education	15 (100%)	20 (100%)
Personal characteristics	14 (95%)	20 (100%)
– Personality and skills	10 (75%)	20 (100%)
– Investigative mind-set	12 (80%)	18 (92%)
– Stereotypes and prejudices	13 (85%)	17 (87%)
– Professional motivation and attitude	12 (80%)	17 (87%)
– Background and life experience	10 (70%)	14 (68%)
– Confidence, reputation and integrity	7 (50%)	16 (80%)
– Mental state during investigation	5 (30%)	5 (27%)
– Intuition	4 (27%)	0 (-)

hours—there is absolutely no room for mistakes', 'The reputation of the entire Norwegian police force is resting on your shoulders when you investigate a high profile murder case'),

4. internal pressure/organisational issues (e.g. 'High workload and pressure from above to "wrap up the case" do not stimulate thoroughness and open-mindedness', 'If an early suspect already is arrested when you arrive at the station it is not an easy decision to let him go, no matter how weak the evidence'), and time pressure

Again, the degree of consensus between British and Norwegian detectives was very high for the majority of situational factors. Only two factors, the role of the defence lawyer and review and revisions, separated the groups by more than 20%.

Individual factors: The categories of responses relating to the qualities of the individual detective were combined into three themes (Table 6.1), corresponding to detective experience (e.g. 'Experience is your best friend but sometimes also your worst enemy. You constantly have to challenge your own assumptions – that is a very hard thing to do'), training and education (e.g. 'The detective training, and indeed the focus of the trainer, can make remarkable differences in how detectives perform in an actual murder case'), and personal characteristics (e.g. 'An investigative mind-setisvital. This is the ability to separate between potential evidence and irrelevant information and at the same time challenge the weight and relevance of your evidence').

The consensus between British and Norwegian participants concerning individual factors was again very high, with the exception of the importance of the detective's intuition. Intuition was not mentioned as a positive asset by any of the British officers, whereas more than one-fourth of the Norwegian officers did so. In contrast, several British officers explicitly warned against the reliance on intuition (e.g. 'Murder investigation should not be based on intuition', 'The detective's gut feeling is normally useless'); these statements were coded as investigative mindset.

It has previously been pointed out that police officers are typically uninformed about essential research findings on human cognition and cognitive biases (Stelfox and Pease 2005). Although this may well be the case, the current findings point to the possibility that experienced detectives seem to develop lay notions which in many cases correspond well with the available research literature. The results of the current study provide support for the applicability of Gollwitzer's (1990) theory of action phases in homicide investigations. British and Norwegian detectives consistently identified two specific types of investigative decisions— (a) decisions to identify, arrest, or charge a suspect and (b) decisions on strategies, hypotheses and lines of inquiry—as particularly likely to act as decisional tipping points, i.e. trigger unconscious and narrowing shifts in mindset. Although the two types of decisions were reported as distinct and separate, they are obviously related. One important aspect of this relationship, which may be explored in future studies, is its temporal dynamics. For instance, the decision to arrest a suspect is very likely to proceed and force decisions on investigative strategies in a particular direction (i.e. focus on the suspect), because of the limited time frame during which the arrest can be sustained. Hence, many times these decisions are perhaps best seen as concatenated and mutually reinforcing, rather than separate and independent. Moreover, because the current study used a purely explorative approach, our data do not permit any conclusions about the actual impact of these tipping points.

STUDY II

The aim of Study II was to test and compare police officers' ability to make high-quality investigative decisions and to resist the influence of decisional tipping points (see Study I). A quasi-experiment compared experienced detectives and novice police officers from England and Norway—two countries with markedly different system for professional qualification. A total of 124 police officers took part in the experiment. They were recruited from four different professional groups: newly educated Norwegian police officers ($n=31$), highly experienced Norwegian homicide detectives ($n=32$), newly educated British police officers ($n=30$), and highly experienced British homicide detectives accredited as senior investigating officers ($n=31$). Participants were presented with two vignettes describing cases where a person had gone missing, which could potentially be construed as homicide cases. The presence of decisional tipping-points (Fahsing and Ask 2013), was manipulated by adding a sentence at the end of the vignette stating that an arrest had been made in the case. After reading each case, participants were asked to identify and write down all necessary and relevant investigative hypotheses and actions. They were not allowed to use any means of assistance and were under observation given 30 minutes to individually conclude on each case. The quality of participants' responses was assessed using an exhaustive gold-standard list of plausible hypotheses and actions. The golden standard was created using a Delphi process (Hsu and Sandford 2007; Linstone and Turoff 1975) where a panel of 15 British and 15 Norwegian senior experts in homicide investigations were asked to identify all necessary investigative hypotheses and investigative actions through a collaborative and iterative process.

There was no significant effect of the manipulated decisional tipping-point on the number of generated gold-standard hypotheses or investigative actions, nor did the tipping-point factor interact with participants' level of experience. However, a clear and significant pattern in the form of a Country × Experience interaction emerged. The experienced officers from England significantly outperformed any other group in the experiment across all measures. The Norwegian bachelor educated novices, with only one year of professional experience, performed slightly better than the experienced Norwegian homicide detectives, and significantly outperformed their UK (novice) counterparts.

Overall, the more experienced participants in our study generated more alternative explanations and investigative actions than did the less experienced police officers (see Table 6.2). A beneficial function of professional experience was, however, only observed among English officers. All participants across all groups favoured hypotheses implying a crime (homicide or kidnap) over non-criminal hypotheses such as suicide or accident. There was no room for such discrimination in the vignettes. In an abductive test of proportional likelihood it is of course crucial to the validity of the investigation that all competing explanations are included from the outset. In practice disproving non-criminal alternatives is sometimes the only way to warrant a so-called 'no body–murder' investigation or a murder charge.

Ideally, all of them should have been generated from the outset and tested on an equal basis. Only 3% of the experienced Norwegian homicide detectives produced all 6 non-criminal hypotheses in the two cases. In one of the cases, even the best performing professional group (accredited English SIO's) generated less than 50% of the non-crime hypotheses including suicide, accident, or sudden illness. Although we did not measure detective decision-making effectiveness directly or in full operational scale, the relevant literature suggests that an adequate generation of relevant hypotheses (i.e., what to investigate) and investigative actions (i.e., how to investigate) is crucial to the outcome of criminal investigations

Table 6.2 Mean proportion of generated gold-standard hypotheses and investigative actions as a function of country, experience, and presence of tipping-point

Country and experience	No tipping-point		s-point	
	M	SD	M	SD
Gold-standard hypotheses[a]				
England				
Novices	.30	.19	.28	.13
Experienced	.36	.25	.78	.25
Norway				
Novices	.52	.23	.50	.23
Experienced	.51	.24	.41	.21
Gold-standard investigative actions[b]				
England				
Novices	.38	.11	.40	.13
Experienced	.73	.14	.73	.13
Norway				
Novices	.62	.15	.60	.14
Experienced	.62	.13	.64	.13

[a]Values represent the proportion of generated gold-standard hypotheses out of the possible maximum
[b]Values represent the proportion of generated gold-standard investigative actions out of the possible maximum

and reduces the risk of cognitive biases (Alison et al. 2013; Ask 2006; Macquet 2009; Nickerson 1998; Simon 2012). The results did not support our prediction that the decision to arrest a suspect would act as an investigative tipping-point (Fahsing and Ask 2013). That is, contrary to expectations, the participating police officers did not overall generate fewer relevant investigative hypotheses and actions in the case where an arrest had (vs. had not) been made, and this tendency was not moderated by officers' level of expertise. This null finding may accurately reflect that strategic decisions, such as making an arrest, exert little influence on investigators' hypothesis generation and testing. On the other hand, at least two circumstances in the current experiment may have reduced the chances of observing such an effect. Firstly, the manipulation of tipping-points was subtle—a single sentence embedded in a larger vignette. Unfortunately, there was no manipulation check to verify that participants actually picked up on this piece of information, so the salience of the manipulation remains unclear. In real-life investigations, such critical decisions are unlikely to go unnoticed.

Secondly, participants were not involved in making the arrest decision, but instead read about a decision already made by a colleague. Thus, participants had little or no personal involvement in the decision, and they did not experience the transition from pre-decisional deliberation to post-decisional implementation. It could be argued, then, that the current experiment bore little resemblance to the types of decisions originally considered by Gollwitzer et al. (1990) in their definition of decision phases.

Our findings suggest that professional experience may improve the ability to generate and test investigative hypotheses in criminal investigators. Overall, the more experienced participants in our study generated more alternative explanations and investigative actions than did the less experienced police officers. The beneficial role of experience was, however, only observed in the English (and not in the Norwegian) sample; experienced Norwegian detectives did not perform any better on our experimental task than did their inexperienced colleagues. Our findings imply that expertise, but only when developed under propitious circumstances, improves the quality of investigative decision-making. To understand why English and Norwegian police officers may benefit differentially from investigative experience, it is useful to recall the differences between the two systems. As a consequence of the Professionalising Investigation Programme (PIP), the English police have a standardised four-step qualification system for detectives, comprehensive procedural guidelines, and detailed routines for systematic reviews and knowledge-sharing (Cook and Tattersall 2008; McCrery and Treacy 2012). Furthermore, English SIOs must undergo annual refreshment training. The Norwegian police, in contrast, have neither a nation-wide qualification program for detectives, or standardised requirements for further training. Instead, competence is developed through personal interest, on-the-job-learning, and non-compulsory education.

Of critical importance for the present study, English SIOs receive mandatory training in the generation and documentation of investigative hypotheses and actions, whereas Norwegian detectives do not. It remains for future research to show whether this particular type of training alone accounts for the observed difference in performance, or whether several components of the PIP programme act synergistically to improve performance. The relatively high performance of Norwegian (vs. English) novices also deserves mention. Possibly, this can be attributed to differences in the nature of the basic police training between the countries. Since 2012, Norwegian police recruits receive some training and education with regard to investigative hypothesis generation and testing. Moreover, their academically pitched 3-year Bachelor in Policing may foster the kind of critical thinking skills necessary to perform relatively well to this particular investigative challenge. The shorter, and more practically oriented, foundation training in England may not prepare recruits equally well for the task.

The complete lack of relationship between extensive professional experience and performance in the Norwegian sample may be surprising. However, this is not the first study failing to demonstrate a beneficial role of presumed expertise or detective experience. Alison et al. (2013) recently found that experience alone did not moderate the debilitating influence of time pressure on detectives' decision-making in a simulated rape investigation. Moreover, Ask and Granhag (2005) found that Swedish experienced police investigators were actually less likely than undergraduate university students to consider alternative explanations of findings in a homicide investigation. In clinical settings, some studies have found that increased experience is associated with an unchanged, or even diminished, ability to perform accurate diagnoses among psychotherapists (Dawes 1996) and physicians (Ericsson et al. 2007). Experienced physicians' ability to diagnose rare diseases picked up only after they had undergone a refresher course (Ericsson et al. 2007).

As noted by Dror (2011), further scientific studies of expertise are crucial to understand its 'paradoxical functional degradation' (p. 184), and thereby contribute to the future development of expert performance. To develop true detective expertise, it appears that not only the mere number of years on the job, but also the type of experience gathered on the job is crucial. The results did not support our prediction that the decision to arrest a suspect would act as an investigative tipping point (Fahsing and Ask 2013). That is, contrary to expectations, police officers did not generate fewer relevant investigative hypotheses and actions in the case where an arrest had (vs. had not) been made, and this tendency was not moderated by officers' level of expertise. This null ending may accurately reject that strategic decisions, such as making an arrest, exert little impudence on investigators' hypothesis generation and testing.

We believe, however, that two circumstances in the current experiment may have reduced the chances of observing such an effect. First, the manipulation of tipping points was subtle—a single sentence embedded in a larger case file. Regrettably, we did not include a manipulation check to verify that participants actually picked up on this piece of information, so the salience of the manipulation remains unclear. In real-life investigations, such critical decisions are unlikely to go unnoticed. Second, participants were not involved in making the arrest decision, but instead read about a decision already made by an unknown colleague. Thus, participants had little or no personal involvement in the decision, and they did not experience the transition from pre-decisional deliberation to post-decisional implementation. It could be argued, then, that the current experiment bore little resemblance to the types of decisions originally considered by Gollwitzer et al. (1990) in their definition of decision phases. Interestingly, participants tended to ignore non-criminal explanations of the cases (e.g. suicide, accident), regardless of the presence or absence of an arrest decision. This corresponds well with previous observations of crime and guilt biases among law-enforcement personnel (Innes 2003; Meissner and Kassin 2002; Packer 1968). An obvious limitation with any quasi-experimental and correlational design is the lack of control over variables that co-vary with the treatment variables of interest. In the current study, this limitation pertains to differences between officers both at different levels of experience and of different nationality. As for experience, it was established empirically that variations in age could not account for the observed differences between novices and experts. It cannot be excluded, however, that experts and novices differed in terms of other stable characteristics which, in turn, are related to investigative decision-making ability. It may be that the psychological makeup of police recruits has changed over the 15–20 years that separate novices and experts in our study. Recent developments of the police profession, at least in Norway, have introduced a growing emphasis on lateral thinking and intellectually demanding tasks (Larsson 2010; Weisburd and Neyroud 2011). The modern police may therefore attract more recruits with an aptitude for abstract reasoning than before. Nevertheless, experienced English SIOs performed much better than did Norwegian police novices with a Bachelor's degree. This suggests that higher education alone does not produce detective expertise, but that it might provide a solid fundamental. The potentially confounding variables related to national differences are greater in number, including factors such as professional status and culture. For instance, if senior detectives enjoy a higher social status in England than in Norway, then the superior performance of the English experts may be due to a stronger motivation to appear as an exceptionally good investigator. Moreover, if individuals attracted to the police occupation in England and Norway differ in terms of stable personality characteristics, then it may be that the two groups naturally grow apart over time due to different rates of improvement, independent of differences in training and accreditation (i.e. so-called selection–maturation interaction; Shadish et al. 2002). Both motivation and maturation, however, are unlikely account for the current findings, as none of these factors would predict that experts would perform better than novices in one country (England) and slightly worse in the other (Norway). A final caveat concerns the representativeness of our experimental task for criminal detectives' actual work. Admittedly, the generation and testing of investigative hypotheses represent only one of many skills required of a senior detective (ACPO 2010). There appears to be strong consensus among policing experts, however, that the ability to generate and evaluate alternative explanations is among the core defining features of an expert detective (ACPO 2012; Cook and Tattersall 2008; Simon 2012; Smith and Flanagan 2000; Stelfox and Pease 2005).

In this study, we have demonstrated that professional experience is potentially beneficial to detectives' ability to identify relevant investigative hypotheses and formulate appropriate lines of inquiry. Importantly, however, increased experience does not guarantee expertise or improved performance. Our findings suggest, rather, that the type of basic education, practical training, standardised investigative procedures and formal evaluation that detectives undergo shapes the course of their professional development. The superior performance displayed by the English SIOs raises the question whether other nations would benefit from the introduction of a program for accreditation, training and review similar to that already in place in England. While this cannot be answered on the basis of a single cross-sectional study, our findings do point in this direction. We hope that our study will inspire further, tightly controlled studies on the relative merits of different qualification and quality assurance systems, and inform policymakers seeking to create optimal conditions for the development of detective expertise.

Study I showed that top detectives from two independent jurisdictions in Europe acknowledge the relevance of Gollwitzer's (1990) mindset theory to their professional role. Furthermore, the study identified factors that might act as decisional tipping-points in criminal investigations. The two critical tipping-points, deciding to make an arrest and deciding on investigative strategies, are not atypical or rare decisions in any way— they are decisions that detectives must do every day in order to solve any crime. Awareness of cognitive biases, as displayed by detectives in Study I, may have some protective effect, but it should primarily be seen as a stepping-stone towards more effective debiasing strategies (Tversky and Koehler 1994). To the author's knowledge, Study I was the first study in the investigative area to document and compare detectives' beliefs and knowledge about their own operational decision-making across different legislative systems. Admittedly, the samples surveyed were small and may, thus, not be fully representative of the detective populations in the respective countries. On the other hand, given the very specialised nature of the professional group, it is rare for studies of this type to tap into such large amounts of detective experience. Moreover, the strong consensus in the detectives' responses indicates that our findings indeed represent prevalent views within the detective community. Our findings further indicate that experienced detectives in both England and Norway are aware of many of the risk factors and obstacles to optimal decision-making that exist in criminal investigations.

Compared to almost all other countries has England and Wales come quite far in the development of such applied countermeasures. As described above, the PIP programme was a huge investment made after decades of turmoil surrounding the quality of criminal investigations in England and Wales. The findings of Study II indicate that the investment was worthwhile, as the English SIO accredited officers dramatically outperformed their Norwegian colleagues with similar length of experience. To understand why English and Norwegian police officers may have benefitted so differentially from investigative experience, it is useful to recall the differences between the two systems. The SIOs that are recruited and trained in the UK PIP programme might therefore develop an affinity for abductive thinking, without the term being explicitly used. The Norwegian police, in contrast, have neither a nation-wide qualification programme for detectives, or standardised requirements for further training. Instead, competence is developed through personal interest, on-the-job-learning and non-compulsory education (Politidirektoratet 2013). The complete lack of relationship between professional experience and performance in the Norwegian sample might seem surprising.

However, this is not the first study failing to demonstrate a beneficial role of presumed expertise (Rolf 2004), nor of detective experience.

Alison et al. (2013) found that experience alone did not moderate the debilitating influence of time pressure on detectives' decision-making in a simulated rape investigation. Moreover, Ask and Granhag (2005) found that Swedish experienced police investigators were actually less likely than undergraduate university students to consider alternative explanations of findings in a homicide investigation. In clinical settings, some studies have found that increased experience is associated with an unchanged, or even diminished, ability to perform accurate diagnoses among psychotherapists (Dawes 1996) and physicians (Ericsson et al. 2007). Experienced physicians' ability to diagnose rare diseases picked up only after they had undergone a refresher course (Ericsson et al. 2007). As concluded by Dror (2011) further scientific studies of expertise are crucial to understanding experts' paradoxical functional degradation, and thereby contribute to the future development of expert performance. Hence, to develop true detective expertise, it appears that not only the mere number of years on the job, but also the type of experience gathered on the job is crucial. A deliberate cultivation of reflectiveness rather than impulsivity is what Baron (1985) called 'actively open-minded thinking'. The superior performance displayed by the English SIOs raises the question whether other nations would benefit from the introduction of similar programmes for authorisation, training, and review inspired by that already in place in England and Wales. While this cannot be answered on the basis of a single cross-sectional study, our findings are encouraging in this regard. It should be noted, however, that although the English senior officers outperformed their Norwegian counterparts and the two novice groups in Study II, even they were not able to consistently identify all the competing scenarios defined by the golden standard.

The information given in the vignettes did not provide enough information to rule out any alternatives. There were strong reasons to suspect murder or abduction in both cases, but that did not imply that any of the other alternatives could be excluded from the outset. This shortcoming in an early stage of a major investigation may ultimately ruin the investigation since information needed to test the lacking hypotheses might never be searched for and hence, could get lost forever (Wagenaar et al. 1993).

These findings indicate that although expertise seems to make us better, it cannot alone be trusted to serve as a complete safeguard against fundamental cognitive limitations. Enduring high performance in complex operations cannot only rest on individual competence alone. In order to truly reduce the risk for human errors in critical operations even the most proficient expert should seek support in thoroughly tested protocols and facilitating professional cultures (Graham 2004).

CONCLUSION

The research reported in this thesis might leave an impression that detectives' judgement and decision-making are more prone to errors and biases than other professional groups. There is, however, no basis for such a claim. Instead, one must recognise that criminal investigations are often based on inherently uncertain sources of information, which means that conclusions beyond reasonable doubt cannot be reached. That is not a defeat for professional detectives, but simply a consequence of how the law is meant to be applied in modern democracies (Simon 2012). In 2005, Stelfox and Pease described cognition and detection as 'reluctant bedfellows', and there is no doubt that the British police service has learned that the hard way (Roycroft et al. 2013). A clear and unmistakable message from the government was needed before some of the available knowledge from social sciences was applied (Home Office 2001, 2004). A great deal is known about the sorts of errors human operators make and why they occur (e.g., Elliott 2005; Fraser-Mackenzie et al. 2013; Yates et al. 2003). This research has been applied to a number of diverse domains, such as the finance industry (e.g., Anderson et al. 1993; Holm and Nystedt 2008; Tversky and Kahneman 1986), the aviation industry (e.g., Hutchins 1995; Sexton et al. 2001; Zsambok and Klein 1997), the health sector (e.g., Arkes et al. 1981; Swets 1988; Weber et al. 1993), and in military command (e.g., Crandall et al. 1992; Freund et al. 1985; Ross et al. 2002), yielding substantial improvements in recruitment, training and operations. To develop similar evidence-based interventions for criminal investigation a lot more experimental research is needed—preferably involving practitioners themselves. Ultimately, the main contribution from psychology is not how each officer should best solve each individual case, but rather how the different professional actors in the chain of justice should be recruited, qualified and organised to best serve the challenging task of fair criminal investigation, prosecution and trial. At present, the best available advice, both on an organisational and individual level, is probably to never be too conclusive and always stay somewhat in doubt.

References

ACPO. (2000). *Murder Investigation Manual.* Wyboston, UK: Association of Chief Police Officers.

ACPO. (2005). *Major Incident Room Standardised Administrative Procedures Manual.* Wyboston: Association of Chief Police Officers.

ACPO. (2006). *Murder Investigation Manual.* Wyboston: Association of Chief Police Officers.

ACPO. (2007). *Practice Advice on Critical Incident Management.* Wyboston, UK: Association of Chief Police Officers.

ACPO. (2010). *Skills for Justice: Policing Professional Framework: Senior Investigation Officer.* Wyboston, UK: Association of Chief Police Officers. Retrieved November 20, 2013, from http://www.skillsforjustice-ppf.com/national-roles/?rt_id=1&rg_id=5&r_id=281.

ACPO. (2012). *Practice Advice on Core Investigative Doctrine* (2nd ed.). Wyboston: Association of Chief Police Officers and National Policing Improvement Agency.

Alison, L., & Crego, J. (2008). *Policing Critical Incidents. Leadership and Critical Incident Management.* Cullompton, Devon: Willan Publishing.

Alison, L., Doran, B., Long, M. L., Power, N., & Humphrey, A. (2013). The Effects of Subjective Time Pressure and Individual Differences on Hypotheses Generation and Action Prioritization in Police Investigations. *Journal of Experimental Psychology: Applied, 19*(1), 83–93. https://doi.org/10.1037/a0032148.

Anderson, J. C., Lowe, D. J., & Reckers, P. M. J. (1993). Evaluation of Auditor Decisions: Hindsight Bias Effects and the Expectation Gap. *Journal of Economic Psychology, 14*(4), 711–737. https://doi.org/10.1016/0167-4870(93)90018-G.

Arkes, H. R., Wortmann, R. L., Saville, P. D., & Harkness, A. R. (1981). Hindsight Bias Among Physicians Weighing the Likelihood of Diagnoses. *Journal of Applied Psychology, 66*(2), 252–254. https://doi.org/10.1037/0021-9010.66.2.252.

Ask, K. (2006). *Criminal Investigation: Motivation, Emotion and Cognition in the Processing of Evidence.* Gothenburg: University of Gothenburg, Department of Psychology.

Ask, K., & Alison, L. (2010). Investigators' Decision Making. In P. A. Granhag (Ed.), *Forensic Psychology in Context: Nordic and International Perspectives* (pp. 35–55). Cullompton: Willan.

Ask, K., & Fahsing, I. (2018). Investigative Decision Making. In A. Griffiths & B. Milne (Eds.), *The Psychology of Criminal Investigation. From Theory to Practice* (pp. 52–73). London: Routledge.

Ask, K., & Granhag, P. A. (2005). Motivational Sources of Confirmation Bias in Criminal Investigations: The Need for Cognitive Closure. *Journal of Investigative Psychology and Offender Profiling, 2*(1), 43–63. https://doi. org/10.1002/jip.19.

Ask, K., & Granhag, P. A. (2007a). Hot Cognition in Investigative Judgments: The Differential Influence of Anger and Sadness. *Law and Human Behavior, 31,* 537–551. https://doi.org/10.1007/s10979-006-9075-3.

Ask, K., & Granhag, P. A. (2007b). Motivational Bias in Criminal Investigators' Judgments of Witness Reliability. *Journal of Applied Social Psychology, 37*(3), 561–591. https://doi.org/10.1111/j.1559-1816.2007.00175.x.

Ask, K., Granhag, P. A., & Rebelius, A. (2011). Investigators Under Influence: How Social Norms Activate Goal-Directed Processing of Criminal Evidence. *Applied Cognitive Psychology, 25,* 548–553. https://doi.org/10.1002/acp.1724.

Baron, J. (1985). *Rationality and Intelligence.* Cambridge, UK: Cambridge University Press.

Cook, T., & Tattersall, A. (2008). *Blackstone's Senior Investigating Officers' Handbook.* Oxford: Oxford University Press.

Crandall, B. W., Kyne, M., Miltello, L., & Klein, G. (1992). *Describing Expertise in One-on-One Instruction* (Contract MDA903-91-C-0058). For the U.S. Army Research Institute, Alexandria, VA. Fairborn, OH: Klein Associates.

Dale, A. (1994). Professionalism and the Police. *The Police Journal, 67*(3), 209–218.

Dawes, R. M. (1996). *House of Cards: Psychology and Psychotherapy Built on Myth.* New York: Free Press.

Dror, I. E. (2011). The Paradox of Human Expertise: Why Experts Can Get It Wrong. In N. Kapur (Ed.), *The Paradoxical Brain* (pp. 177–188). Cambridge: Cambridge University Press.

Elliott, T. (2005). *Expert Decision-Making in Naturalistic Environments: A Summary of Research.* Edinburg (Australia): Land Operations Division Systems Sciences Laboratory.

Ericsson, K. A., Prietula, M. J., & Cokely, E. T. (2007). The Making of an Expert. *Harvard Business Review, 85*(7–8), 114–121.

Eyre, M., Crego, J., & Alison, L. (2008). Electronic Debriefs and Simulations as Descriptive Methods for Defining the Critical Incident Landscape. In L. Alison & J. Crego (Eds.), *Policing Critical Incidents.* Cullompton, Devon: Willan Publishing.

Fahsing, I. (2013). Tænkestile: Effektivitet, dyder og krydspress i efterforskninger. In C. Hald & K. V. Rønn (Eds.), *Om at opdage – Metodiske refleksjoner over politiets undersøkelsespraksis* (pp. 117–146). Copenhagen: Samfundslitteratur.

Fahsing, I. A., & Ask, K. (2013). Decision Making and Decisional Tipping Points in Homicide Investigations: An Interview Study of British and Norwegian Detectives. *Journal of Investigative Psychology and Offender Profiling, 10*(2), 155–165. https://doi.org/10.1002/jip.1384.

Fahsing, I. A., & Rachlew, A. A. (2009). Investigative Interviewing in the Nordic Region. In B. Milne & S. Savage (Eds.), *International Developments in Investigative Interviewing* (pp. 39–65). Devon: Willan.

Findley, K. A., & Scott, M. S. (2006). The Multiple Dimensions of Tunnel Vision in Criminal Cases. *Wisconsin Law Review, 291,* 291–397.

Fraser-Mackenzie, P. A. F., Bucht, R., & Dror, I. E. (2013). Forensic Judgement and Decision-Making. In T. R. Zentall & P. H. Crowley (Eds.), *Comparative Decision Making* (pp. 144–153). Oxford: Oxford Scholarship Online.

Freund, T., Kruglanski, A. W., & Schpitzajzen, A. (1985). The Freezing and Unfreezing of Impressional Primacy: Effects of the Need for Structure and the Fear of Invalidity. *Personality and Social Psychology Bulletin, 11*(4), 479–487. https://doi.org/10.1177/0146167285114013.

Gollwitzer, P. M. (1990). Action Phases and Mind-Sets. In E. T. Higgins (Ed.), *Handbook of Motivation and Cognition: Foundations of Social Behavior* (Vol. 2, pp. 53–92). New York, NY: The Guilford Press.

Gollwitzer, P. M., Heckhausen, H., & Steller, B. (1990). Deliberative and Implemental Mind-Sets: Cognitive Tuning Toward Congruous Thoughts and Information. *Journal of Personality and Social Psychology, 59*(6), 1119–1127. https://doi.org/10.1037//0022-3514.59.6.1119.

Graham, C. (2004). Advanced Airway Management in the Emergency Department: What are the Training and Skills Maintenance Needs for UK Emergency Physicians? *Emergency Medicine Journal, 21*(1), 14. https://doi.org/10.1136/emj.2003.003368.

Hald, C. K. (2011). *Web Without a Weaver—On the Becoming of Knowledge: A Study of Criminal Investigation in the Danish Police.* Boca Raton, FL: Universal Publishers.

Hallenberg, K., O'Neill, M., & Tong, S. (2016). Watching the Detectives. In M. Brunger, S. Tong, & D. Martin (Eds.), *Introduction to Policing Research: Taking Lessons From Practice* (p. 101). London, UK: Routledge.

Holm, H., & Nystedt, P. (2008). Trust in Surveys and Games – A Methodological Contribution on the Influence of Money and Location. *Journal of Economic Psychology, 29*(4), 522–542. https://doi.org/10.1016/j.joep.2007.07.010.

Home Office. (2001). *Policing a New Century: A Blueprint for Reform.* London: Home Office.

Home Office. (2004). *National Policing Plan 2004–2007.* London, UK: Home Office.

Hsu, C. C., & Sandford, B. A. (2007). The Delphi Technique: Making Sense Of Consensus in Practical Assessment. *Research & Evaluation, 12*(10), 1–8.

Hutchins, E. (1995). How a Cockpit Remembers its Speeds. *Cognitive Science, 19*(3), 265–288. https://doi.org/10.1207/s15516709cog1903_1.

Innes, M. (2003). *Investigating Murder: Detective Work and the Police Response to Criminal Homicide.* Oxford: Oxford University Press.

James, A., & Mills, M. (2012). Does Acpo Know Best: To What Extent May the Pip Programme Provide a Template for the Professionalisation of Policing? *The Police Journal, 85*(2), 133–149.

Jones, D., Grieve, J., & Milne, B. (2008). The Case to Review Murder Investigations. *The Journal of Homicide and Major Incident Investigation, 2*(4), 51–70. https://doi.org/10.1093/police/pan053.

Larsson, P. (2010). Fra armesterke bondesønner til akademikerbarn [From the Strong Sons of Farmers to the Kids of Intellectuals]. *Nordisk Tidskrift for Kriminalvidenskab, 97*(2), 150–155.

Linstone, H. A., & Turoff, M. (1975). *The Delphi Method: Techniques and Applications.* CA: Addison-Wesley Educational Publishers.

Macquet, A. C. (2009). Recognition Within the Decision-Making Process: A Case Study of Expert Volleyball Players. *Journal of Applied Sport Psychology, 21*, 64–79. https://doi.org/10.1080/10413200802575759.

McGrory, D., & Treacy, P. (2012). The Professionalising Investigation Programme. In M. R. Haberfeld, C. A. Clarke, & D. L. Sheehan (Eds.), *Police Organization and Training: Innovations in Research and Practice* (Vol. 1, pp. 113–137). New York: Springer.

Meissner, C. A., & Kassin, S. M. (2002). "He's Guilty!": Investigator Bias in Judgments of Truth and Deception. *Law and Human Behavior, 26*(5), 469–480. https://doi.org/10.1023/A:1020278620751.

Nickerson, R. S. (1998). Confirmation Bias: A Ubiquitous Phenomenon in Many Guises. *Review of General Psychology, 2*(2), 175–220. https://doi.org/10.1037/1089-2680.2.2.175.

O'Neill, M. (2018). *Key Challenges in Criminal Investigation.* Bristol, UK: Policy Press.

Packer, H. L. (1968). *The Limits of the Criminal Sanction.* Stanford, CA: Stanford University Press.

Persak, N. (2014). *Legitimacy and Trust in Criminal Law, Policy and Justice: Norms, Procedures, Outcomes.* Surrey, UK: Ashgate Publishing, Ltd.

Politidirektoratet. (2013). *Etterforskningen i politiet 2013.* Oslo: Politidirektoratet.

Rachlew, A. A. (2009). *Justisfeil ved politiets etterforskning – noen eksempler og forskningsbaserte mottiltak* (Ph.D.). University of Oslo, Oslo.

Riksadvokaten. (2015). *Norsk politi og påtalemyndighets behandling av straffesakene mot Sture Bergwall – Hva kan vi lære? (3/2015).* Oslo, Norway. http://www.riksadvokaten.no/filestore/Dokumenter/2015/Riksadvokatenspublikasjoner3_2015.pdf.

Rolf, B. (2004). Metod och anarki i praktiken. In C. M. Allwood (Ed.), *Perspektiv på kvalitativ metod*. Lund: Studentlitteratur AB.

Ross, K. G., McHugh, A., Moon, B. M., Klein, G., Armstrong, A. A., & Rall, E. (2002). *High-level Cognitive Processes in Field Research (Year One Final Report und Contract o2TA2-SP1_RT1 for U.S. Army Reserach Laboratory Under Cooperative Agreement DAAD19-01-2-0009)*. Fairborn, OH: Klein Associates Inc.

Rossmo, D. K. (2014). Case Rethinking: A Protocol for Reviewing Criminal Investigations. *Police Practice and Research: An International Journal*. https://doi.org/10.1080/15614263.2014.978320.

Roycroft, M., Brown, J., & Innes, M. (2013). Reform by Crisis: The Murder of Stephen Lawrence and a Socio-historical Analysis of Developments in the Conduct of Major Crime Investigations. In M. Rowe (Ed.), *Policing Beyond Macpherson* (pp. 148–164). Cullompton, UK: Willan Publishing.

Sexton, J. B., Thomas, E. J., & Helmreich, R. L. (2001). Error, Stress, and Teamwork in Medicine and Aviation: Cross Sectional Surveys. *Journal of Human Performance in Extreme Environments*, 6(1). https://doi. org/10.7771/2327-2937.1019.

Shadish, W. R., Cook, T. D., & Campbell, D. T. (2002). *Experimental and Quasi-Experimental Designs for Generalized Causal Inference*. Belmont, CA: Wadsworth.

Simon, D. (2012). *In Doubt: The Psychology of the Criminal Justice Process*. Cambridge, MA: Harvard University Press.

Smith, N., & Flanagan, C. (2000). *The Effective Detective: Identifying the Skills of an Effective SIO* (Police Research Series Paper 122). London: Policing and Reducing Crime Unit.

Stelfox, P., & Pease, K. (2005). Cognition and Detection: Reluctant Bedfellows? In M. J. Smith & N. Tilley (Eds.), *Crime Science: New Approaches to Preventing and Detecting Crime* (pp. 191–207). Cullompton: Willan.

Swets, J. A. (1988). Measuring the Accuracy of Diagnostic Systems. *Science*, 240(4857), 1285–1293. https://doi.org/10.1126/science.3287615.

Tong, S. (2009). Assessing Performance: Quantity of Quality? In S. Tong, R. P. Bryant, & M. Horvarth (Eds.), *Understanding Criminal Investigation*. Chichester, UK: Wiley.

Tversky, A., & Kahneman, D. (1986, October). Rational Choice and the Framing of Decisions. *The Journal of Business*, 59 (No. 4, Part 2: The Behavioral Foundations of Economic Theory), 251–278. https://doi. org/10.1086/296365.

Tversky, A., & Koehler, D. J. (1994). Support Theory: A Nonextensional Representation of Subjective Probability. *Psychological Review, 101*(4).

Wagenaar, W. A., van Koppen, P. J., & Crombag, H. F. M. (1993). *Anchored Narratives: The Psychology of Criminal Evidence*. New York: St. Martin's Press.

Weber, E. U., Böckenholt, U., Hilton, D. J., & Wallace, B. (1993). Determinants of Diagnostic Hypothesis Generation: Effects of Information, Base Rates, and Experience. *Journal of Experimental Psychology: Learning, Memory, and Cognition, 19,* 1151–1164. https://doi.org/10.1037//0278-7393.19.5.1151.

Weisburd, D., & Neyroud, P. (2011, January). *Police Science: Towards a New Paradigm.* Paper Presented at the National Institute of Justice/Harvard University Executive Session on Policing and Public Safety, Harvard Kennedy School, Cambridge, MA.

Westera, N. J., Kebbell, M. R., Milne, B., & Green, T. (2014). Towards a More Effective Detective. *Policing and Society: An International Journal of Research and Policy.* https://doi.org/10.1080/10439463.2014.912647.

Yates, J. F., Veinott, E. S., & Patalano, A. L. (2003). Hard Decisions, Bad Decisions. In S. L. Schneider & J. C. Shanteau (Eds.), *Emerging Perspectives on Judgement and Decision Research* (pp. 13–63). New York: Cambridge University Press.

Zsambok, C. E., & Klein, G. (Eds.). (1997). *Naturalistic Decision Making.* Hillsdale, NJ, England: Lawrence Erlbaum Associates, Inc.

CHAPTER 7

The Task Is Greater Than the Title: Professionalising the Role of the Senior Investigating Officer in Homicide Investigations

Declan Donnelly and Adrian West

Abstract The authors argue that the Police should acknowledge that the basic premise of a professional organisation lies in having an appropriate corpus of professional knowledge. The attainment of knowledge as a necessary foundation for the discipline and practice of investigation requires a radical change to the current training and development of investigators. The development of Senior Investigating Officers (SIO) expertise should be recognised as requiring the summation of relevant theoretical and conceptual domain knowledge, enhanced decision-making skills and the accumulation of investigative experience that allows ready access to

D. Donnelly
Faculty of Arts, Humanities and Social Sciences, Anglia Ruskin University, Cambridge, UK

A. West (✉)
Liverpool Centre for Advanced Policing Studies,
Liverpool John Moore's University, Liverpool, UK

© The Author(s) 2019   107
M. Roycroft and J. Roach (eds.),
Decision Making in Police Enquiries and Critical Incidents,
https://doi.org/10.1057/978-1-349-95847-4_7

conceptual and practical models for action. An understanding of how other disciplines can assist the investigative process requires more than a superficial familiarity with their methods. The emphasis should be on the acquisition of critical thinking and complex problem-solving skills.

Keywords The influence of the practices of the past · The acquisition of knowledge · 'Good coppering' versus human factors · Sense making · Investigative expertise · Investigative theory

> Last home, first in. Relentless. Absolutely committed to finding the murderer. When he walked into the briefing room, everyone stood up. He was stern but he knew that shaming or humiliating someone doesn't motivate them. Thorough. He wanted to hear every view because he was experienced enough to know that his leadership would not be undermined or challenged by what he heard. He was also thorough because he never assumed that just because someone said that they had done something, it didn't mean that it was as thorough as he would have conducted it. So, he would say, in front of the briefing, talk me through that interview with that witness. They called him the man with no shadow. (Notes about an SIO,[1] 1994)

INTRODUCTION

The practitioner and academic experiences of the authors provide the basis for the content of this chapter. One a non-police officer and "outsider" as a Forensic Clinical Psychologist providing investigative advice to Senior Investigating Officers (SIO) and the other as a former SIO and "insider" now researching decision-making by SIOs in stranger homicide investigations. That experience spans over twenty years of involvement in major incident rooms, beginning in the 1990s, during a period when a shortage of experienced SIO's was also accompanied by appeals to Advice on Core Investigative Doctrine (ACPO) to support detective selection, training and career progression to develop the SIO's of the future (Smith and Flanagan 2000). As the opening observation

---

[1] Verbatim comments of a detective constable about a SIO recorded by AGW Dr. Adrian West, December 1994.

indicates, we are aware of many outstanding men and women who as SIOs have demonstrated sound investigative reasoning alongside unrelenting effort and unknown costs to their physical and emotional health. Nevertheless, it is our view that the investigative capability of the Police Service generally and the art and science of homicide investigation specifically requires significant development and improvement. Almost two decades on from Smith and Flanagan (2000), the HMIC (2017, p. 12) echoes our concerns, stating, "… there is a national crisis in the severe shortage of investigators." Although the SIO is not referred to explicitly, the issue of poor supervision is emphasised: "For some time, HMIC has been concerned about the supervision of criminal investigations. Poor or inconsistent supervision means that too many cases do not make the progress that they should and too many of those investigating crimes do not develop their skills sufficiently. Good supervision is also vital for staff welfare" (HMIC 2017, p. 13). As some forces struggle to recruit and develop detectives, the HMIC also appears increasingly aware that "those who lack appropriate skills and experience" may be leading complex investigations. As we attempt to show, such observations have been repeated frequently across the years. We anticipate that they are likely to continue until the training and development of the police investigator are radically improved and the role truly professionalised.

The Influence of the Practices of the Past

… be aware of the undoubted fact that sophisticated and brutal criminals will continue to be caught, in the first instance, not by devices but by the trained, discriminating and humane eye, the persevering determination and the dedication of ordinary police officers, determined to keep the streets as free from the obscenity and eventual degradation of crime as is possible. Get to the truth, then, it stands all tests. (Powis 1977, p. 170)

It is our impression that the current culture and practice of police investigative work is still influenced by conduct and attitudes that emanated from a time when the notion of "professional expertise" relied on the dominance of practical situational experience over any other basis for investigative decision making. That dominance of practical situational experience could be generalised and encapsulated in an attitude that declared, "Nothing can be taught, it can only be understood if it has been witnessed". In police investigative practice, this was mostly enshrined in the notion of apprenticeship to an experienced guide (Irving and Dunnighan 1993, p. 23). Numerous accounts attest that for some, that journey often appeared to incorporate the pub as much as the courtroom (Forbes 1973; Hobbs 1988).

There are some notable biographies that described the role that the novice, guided by a more experienced detective, was expected to perform to learn the craft and "folklore" of detective work. du Rose (1971, p. 17) in his memoirs recalled that his initial CID training was to be paired with an experienced detective in order to learn the "trade". The qualities required of an investigator relied on the ability to "build a chain of informants" and to possess a "cunning" that matched those of the "crooks". It was essential for a lead investigator to have the "loyalty" of their staff (p. 109). Forbes (1973) provided a similar account of his transition to the CID, which was not marked by any formal training but took place over a period during which he was "apprenticed" to an experienced detective (p. 5). He described one aspect of detective ability as the requirement of "knowing" what is taking place on the "division", which was developed by "drinking in public houses" (p. 22). This social process assisted with the cultivation of informants and was viewed by peers and supervisors as important in the development of detective ability (p. 44). A murder squad detective required, "the art of being a good thief catcher and hard knowledge of criminals" (p. 34).

Hobbs' (1988) "partial" analysis of detective work based on his ethnographic inquiry and "informal" access to a limited section of the police organisation also illustrates the centrality of "pubs and clubs" and "the heavy drinking sessions" in times past. It was in these situations that the trading of information occurred between detectives and those either involved or on the edges of criminality. To be able to obtain information and develop informants was seen as the staple of the detective craft. It was actively encouraged by senior Criminal Investigation Departments (CID) management and is what Hobbs (1988) sublimely refers to as the "entrepreneurial" essence of the detective. The experience of both authors also includes hangovers as well as memories of male-dominated CID ("the department"; Mark 1978, p. 122) when, for good or ill, some detectives appeared to operate with a sense of superiority and entitlement that was rooted less to their role and purpose and more to their sense of belonging to "a force within a force" and "a club within a club". Those who found themselves excluded 'in uniform' and without any hope of ever gaining that subsequent career long membership and its supposed attendant status, were often more aggrieved because of the operation of open patronage and the informal selection procedures of whichever clique influenced admission. Both in the Metropolitan districts as well as "the provinces" it was well known that for some departments, membership was based around informal criteria that sometimes included proficiency at a particular sport as much as being "a good thief taker". Inevitably, such exclusion sometimes created resentment towards members of "departments" and consequent limitations to their development and careers.

A review of the impact of corruption is beyond the scope of this chapter. Nevertheless, it is acknowledged that corruption and inefficiency contributed to a long period beginning with the Maxwell Confait case in the early 1960s which was marked by high-profile cases that highlighted ineffective investigative processes, failures in leadership, lack of effective management and inadequate training of officers at all ranks, but particularly that of the SIO. Others have argued that the investigative reforms that arose from these cases failed to address the "systemic tensions" that can arise in difficult to solve enquiries (Roycroft et al. 2007, p. 150). We suggest that those "systemic tensions" are a reflection of the lack of an "accepted corpus of knowledge" in the police service with regard to the investigation of crime (Stelfox and Pease 2005, p. 192). Instead, the tradition of investigation had been passed on through the collective sharing of stories and the practicalities of doing the job (West 2001), or as Hobbs (1988) has aptly stated, a matter of, "Doing the Business".[2]

Stelfox (2007) has also suggested that the role of the investigator must be professionalised so as to move from the perception of a craft to recognition of a profession similar to the model of professional practice that underpins other occupational groups such as nursing or social work. As he points out, unlike the true professions such as Medicine or the Law, the police service and particularly the investigative function have only a limited professional literature to which they can refer. How then can investigative practice assume the mantle of a profession? To be considered a profession Schon (1983, p. 34), states that the development

---

[2]We acknowledge that Hobbs' description of the CID of the 1980s as having, "an essentially organisationally deviant persona" is virtually unrecognisable when set against today's arrangements for investigating crime. Since few crime investigation departments exist, we suggest that it will be difficult to identify many of the instances that Hobbs described.

of an "instrumental practice" is essential. This denotes that there is an epistemology of practice that distinguishes the profession as being based upon rigorous practical knowledge as opposed to that which is comprised of "craft and artistry".

THE ACQUISITION OF KNOWLEDGE

Forty years ago, "when books of practice are rare in police literature," (Stead 1977, p. xii) David Powis a Deputy Assistant Commissioner in the Criminal Investigation Department of New Scotland Yard, wrote a "Field Manual for Police". At a time when "patrol" was understood as "the basic function" and "front line" of detective and uniformed police work, he emphasised "vigilance" or "watchfulness" as a "primary police quality" (Stead 1977, p. xi). The manual, which essentially comprises guidance about "knowing what to watch for ... in practical street work", provides many instances of so-called "acquirable skills" (Powis 1977, p. 1). We acknowledge that such a craft training approach might have been a necessary adaptation to previous circumstances. Indeed, we acknowledge that persistence, dedication and commitment to an overarching moral responsibility are integral to the investigation of crime. However, Powis's endorsement that police work is about intuition, gut feeling and hunches provokes more concern about negative influences, if indeed it accurately reflected the dominant investigative attitude of that time: "Try not to be over-reluctant to act upon 'hunches', for they are probably based upon quite sensible prior observation, taken in and registered by your brain within a minute fraction of a second" (Powis 1977, p. 1).

"GOOD COPPERING" VERSUS HUMAN FACTORS

"No need for fancy forensic science or clever psychological profile: just 'good coppering' of the sort that every policeman believes they are capable".

"There is", [the Detective Superintendent] opines, "no such thing as the perfect murder. Killers are by and large amateurs. It is the detectives who are the professionals. It is we who understand the business of murder" (Tate and Wyre 1992, p. 209).

Almost twenty-five years ago, Tate and Wyre (1992) following a murder squad for a television documentary and an accompanying book, appeared to reveal a persistent insistence on the superiority of "good coppering" for the investigation of murder. Ten years previously, in the fall out from the Yorkshire Ripper investigation, Byford had asserted (though admittedly with reference to multiple murder cases that cross force boundaries), that the traditional attributes of the senior detective including, "professional expertise, a sound knowledge of the criminal law and practice and a capacity for assembling evidence" are not enough and that a different skill set is required (Byford 1981, pp. 371–372).

Others were attempting during that period to shed light on how to improve that investigative skill set. Notably, Irving and Dunnighan (1993) in their research on behalf of the Royal Commission on Criminal Justice highlighted the human factors that are involved in formulating a case to the required standard of proof to be prosecuted within the judicial system. Again, in contrast to the "craftlike" conception of detective work, they understood the CID system as "entirely devoted to the processing of complex information" (1993, p. 1). They suggested the process from acquisition of identifying a suspect through to arrest and charge requires the use of "higher order" cognitive skills (p. 8) involving memory, acuity, vigilance and reasoning. The reasoning process requires the detective to access a "range of logico-deductive activities" (p. 16). They recognised that not all these skills are well developed in individuals (p. 13).

Their study identified areas of concern in relation to procedure and errors in understanding and applying the Police and Criminal Evidence Act, 1984 (PACE), divergence from CID procedure and errors in continuity of evidence. Common causes of individual error were identified as the failure to deduce that certain consequences damaging to a case would occur as a result of the decisions taken. They recommended, inter alia, that training should be introduced for detectives and managers into the errors they are likely to make, the conditions in which error is likely to occur and the means by which errors can be reduced.

Nevertheless, in spite of their recommendations, the primary source of SIO knowledge twenty-five years ago remained essentially experiential. The teaching method on courses for SIOs was predominantly a case study approach of high-profile serious and series cases. Arguably, the values about what seemed to make a good detective were passed down through war stories and storytelling—shared stories of policing (Innes 2003; Reiner 2010). There were no formal lectures on decision-making or the possible causes of error. The moral responsibility of the SIO remained predominant, exemplified by the opening introduction to the

SCIMITAR course: "No greater honour can be bestowed upon an investigator than investigating the death of a fellow human being". Entry on to the SCIMITAR course at the Police Staff College, which no longer exists, required demonstrable experience as a Detective Chief Inspector. This again reflected the value that was placed on years of experience in the CID ahead of other abilities.

In the intervening period, investigative practice has been supported by investigator handbooks such as that written by Brookman (2005) dealing with all aspects of homicide, and Cook and Tattersall's (2016) compendium of the do's and don'ts of investigative practice. The introduction of manuals such as the Murder Investigation Manual (MIM) (ACPO 2006), the Guidance on Major Incident Room Standardised Administrative Procedures (MIRSAP) (ACPO 2005a) and the Practice ACPO (2005b) have evolved from failures identified in various high profile investigations (Byford 1981; MacPherson 1999; Sentamu et al. 2002; Smith 2003; Flanagan 2004). The Core Investigative Doctrine, for example, emphasises the value to the investigator of the investigative mindset, so as to avoid the types of cognitive bias that may unduly influence the thinking processes of the investigator. The MIM, which is presented as a scientific model of investigation dealing with various phases of investigative procedure, is also an attempt to produce a comprehensive theory of investigation. However, whilst it is presented as a science-based approach to investigation, it is also a template to ensure that routine procedures and checklists are completed. Consequently, it may be more suited to the experienced investigator than the trainee (Tong et al. 2009). The basic problem as we have repeated and Bryant (2009) again argues is that even with the MIM as guidance, there is still no commonly accepted corpus of knowledge to inform the process of detection. As opposed to an art and craft approach based upon a hunches and intuition, Bryant views a science of investigation as that based upon inquisitorial, truth-seeking as against the common law adversarial stance.

Tong (2009) also reminds us that there is a distinction between training and education. Training constitutes the acquisition of skills through the learning of police procedure and then being able to perform the task required of a police officer. Education in contrast is focused on research, and is coupled with the cognitive ability to categorise, evaluate and understand. This also incorporates receptiveness to learning new facts and concepts and the ability to communicate differing perspectives effectively both orally and in writing. Education is therefore about lifelong long learning and is not a short-term fix.

THE PHASES AND PRESSURES
OF HOMICIDE INVESTIGATION TODAY

In the UK, the investigation of crime involves a separation of powers between the various parties involved in the criminal justice process. The Police investigate; the Crown Prosecution Service (CPS) decide whether there is sufficient evidence to prosecute; the Judge in a criminal trial at Crown Court directs the jury on the law; the Jury decide all matters of fact and proof.[3] The function of the police in a criminal investigation is to impartially gather and present evidential material to the CPS and the defence (Stelfox 2009). Although crimes vary in terms of their complexity, the investigative process typically follows a sequence of phases: In response to the reporting of a crime, the initial investigative phase involves clarification of the circumstances and the early retrieval of evidence and intelligence. In what Innes (2007, p. 255) describes as the identifying and acquiring stage, it is this decision-making within the first 24–72 hours about what is considered relevant or irrelevant information, which often forms the basis for the subsequent success or failure of an investigation (Oughton 1971; Bruhns 1982; Tate and Wyre 1992; Stelfox 2009). This phase ideally involves a degree of "openness" and willingness to consider a range of investigative possibilities; otherwise "premature closure" with all of its attendant risks may ensue (Savage and Milne 2007, pp. 614–615).

The evaluation phase should follow, involving the "interpreting and understanding" of evidence and intelligence to generate the inferences and hypotheses which will then form the basis for further investigations (Innes 2007). Consequently, awareness of any gaps or conflicts in investigative knowledge should allow actions to be prioritised to secure further evidence for analysis and interpretation. This is an iterative process as the investigative team continues to compile critical facts to either implicate or eliminate individuals from an inquiry. This phase of the process often involves a close involvement by forensic scientists to input into the whole range of investigative problems.

The investigative team also begin to establish "narrative coherence" from the considerable amount of material gained during their investigation (Innes 2002b). Innes (2003) observes that detectives in dealing

[3]Lord MacDonald QC. 2015. Interview. In: *Today Programme*. BBC Radio 4. 22 May. 07:15 hrs.

with murder utilise typologies, including, for example, an argument-related death, or death at the hands of a stranger. These typologies are a form of investigative "heuristic". They are an identifiable way of describing murders that are a product of the shared experience of those investigating murder. This provides an extant sense of what occurred during the fatal interaction between the parties. In doing so it enables detectives to understand how to "do" policing and reduces the complexities of investigation so that it is "negotiated" and "ordered" (Innes 2002a, p. 69). In those homicide types that are not usually encountered, lack of typologies or working models to make sense of the out of the ordinary can significantly hinder that appraisal. Sense-making is a form of investigative heuristic or cognitive "shortcut" through which the observer understands crime scenes. Through this process, they begin the interpretation of what occurred and the interaction of victims and witnesses (Stelfox and Pease 2005, p. 192). The readiness to seek and incorporate the guidance of others who may have more relevant investigative knowledge cannot be assumed at this stage. Without specialist (including evidence based) knowledge of typologies of offenders and offences, naïve theories (Baron 2008) about the formulation of a case can sometimes significantly hinder investigative progress.

The next phase occurs after the arrest and interview of a suspect. There begins the selection, ordering and presentation of investigative material. Savage and Milne (2007, pp. 614–615) caution that even at this stage the investigator must maintain a critical mindset and not close down investigative options. They refer to this as a shift from establishing what has occurred to "knowing" what has happened. Starting then from a "premise of guilt" the evidence is pieced together in a format that can be understood and interpreted by both judge and jury (Hobbs 1988). In his analysis of the manner in which detectives assemble and prepare a case for court, Carson (2007, p. 412) suggests that the current investigative paradigm is focused primarily on the product of the investigation, namely that of prosecution and conviction. This narrow focus he argues can lead to "precipitous decision making or premature conclusions" where not all investigative possibilities have been considered. Other researchers have argued that it is at this point when the focus of an investigation is primarily centred on one suspect, to the detriment of other alternative possibilities, that has led to miscarriages of justice (Leo 2008; Simon 2012; Kassin 2012).

The idea of a case being assembled and created as a story with a beginning, middle and end assist those who decide upon the facts, the jury. They can then readily understand what has occurred (Innes 2002b, 2003). The fact that a person is charged does not mean that the case is concluded. The case management still requires the evidence to be overseen and further police inquiries may still be required (Sentamu et al. 2002; Stelfox 2007). Thus, knowledge of the law and how to utilise the legal framework is considered essential to detective work. For example, being able to distinguish between the essential legal elements of the offence of murder and manslaughter will impact on how a case may be constructed (Innes 2002a; Stelfox 2009). In a similar way, the Court process may dominate an SIO's thinking to the extent that his or her decision-making process is focused on the requirement to ensure that any possible defences are pre-empted or negated (Brookman and Innes 2013). The investigation of murder is a challenging event for any SIO. In their analysis of investigative thinking styles Dean et al. (2006), suggest that the more difficult the crime the increased level of thinking style is required to solve it. Ultimately, the SIO will face intense scrutiny in examination and cross-examination about their direction and any aspect of their decision-making across all phases of an investigation in a range of possible judicial tribunals.

The Pressures on a SIO

Therefore, critical to the effectiveness of an investigation is the role and leadership of the SIO. Deferential references to "the governor" or "the boss", may be heard far less frequently these days, and the "autocratic" SIO may well be an artefact of the past, but have no doubt, the SIO remains the nucleus of an investigation. The responsibility for the success or failure of an investigation still rests upon his or her shoulders (West and Alison 2005, p. 385).

The range of investigative, organisational and managerial responsibilities and consequent pressures facing a SIO should not be underestimated. They will vary depending upon the complexity of the murder that is under investigation. These responsibilities include meeting the needs of the victim's family and the ability to provide leadership and direction to all the various teams in the investigation. Amongst all of this, the SIO must navigate a myriad of internal police policies and external legislation. In particular, they must comply with the procedures and policies of the organisation as set out in the MIM (2006) and MIRSAP (2005a). Moreover, they must possess a knowledge of the law in relation to homicide and how the application of investigative legislation, such as the Regulation of Investigatory Powers Act 2000 (RIPA) and the Criminal Proceedings and Investigation Act 1996 (CPIA) can be applied to their investigation.

Additionally, as a hierarchical organisation, the Police Service creates its own internal pressures on the SIO. These include senior management's role in accounting for the cost and resourcing of an enquiry. The longer an enquiry takes, the more such hierarchical intrusion will be evident as the pressure on the investigator to "get a result" mounts (Innes 2002b, p. 676; Alison et al. 2013). The views of Gold (command) and external advisory groups can combine with internal review procedures to produce a level of oversight that can be perceived as undermining rather than supportive. The role of the IPCC can on occasions also add to a perception of threat in what can be experienced as a very lonely, isolated and vulnerable position. Other forms of pressure also emerge particularly if the enquiry becomes protracted over many months or in rare cases, over years (Byford 1981). Informally ascribed opinions from canteen or corridor discussions about how good an SIO is thought to be from either his or her peers and from within the murder investigation team do not always go unheard.

We acknowledge that when set against this array of pressures, the gold standard of a hypothetico-deductive-empirical approach to a murder enquiry, may be easily compromised. Such optimal circumstances for decision-making assume that all information and intelligence is accessible and can be straightforwardly analysed. We also acknowledge the reality of those occasions when political and organisational forces can impact and impede upon the most rational approach to any investigative process. Nevertheless, given the complexity of the task, the scale of the responsibility and accountability, and the training and development that underpins the role of other similar professional groups, we believe that the current piecemeal approach to the training and development of SIOs can no longer be justified. This view is not ours alone. Others have also arrived at the same conclusion that detective training requires improvement in a move away from "craft" towards a scientific foundation of investigation (Tong 2009). This involves the development of an investigative theory where investigative knowledge and practice are based upon the learning and application of the scientific method to investigation.

Such development necessarily includes, for example, formal instruction in reasoning and logic, and understanding of relevant theoretical knowledge (Carson 2009, 2013). As opposed to what previous critics have identified as far too much emphasis on law and procedures (Irving and McKenzie 1993; Maguire 2008; West 2001; Tong 2009).

THE DEVELOPMENT OF THE COMPETENT SIO

Concern regarding the effectiveness of those leading complex investigations has not just been confined to high-profile cases. The Royal Commission on Criminal Justice recommended that those conducting investigations must be properly trained so as to avoid the errors most frequently made during investigations (Runciman 1993, p. 9). This criticism was acknowledged by the Home Office and the Police Service and subsequently, various studies under the aegis of the then Police Research Group were undertaken to determine the qualities required to function as an effective investigating officer.

Significantly, Adhami and Browne (1996) examined the expertise of detectives investigating child sexually oriented homicide. The rarity of this offence, less than 10% of all murders, means that the scope for detectives to build a repertoire of experience is limited when compared with the investigation of "domestic" murder (more than 90%) (p. 15). In dealing with crimes of this nature any "know how" will depend upon the experience derived from investigating other murders. This will be supplemented by knowledge gained through "informal networks". The inherent danger in this form of social processing is that exchanges in relation to how a case was solved may be misunderstood due to this informality. Additionally, the information imparted by the holder of the "knowledge" may be selective or have been retrospectively rationalised (p. 14). The lack of experience in dealing with these more complex cases and the reliance on the knowledge of others lead Adhami and Browne to suggest that the inference layer of "detectives expertise is weak" (p. 21). This may be the first study of its kind in the UK to examine in an investigative context the reasoning processes of SIO's. They suggest that their findings are applicable to other murders particularly those cases where the ability to develop inferential rules are greater due to the higher volume of cases dealt with by an SIO (p. 23).

Their suggestion to redress the gaps in investigator knowledge is a specifically defined course of training and reading. In support of this they cite Kind (1987). He not only advocated the introduction of a training course based upon scientific methods of investigation, but also importantly sought to distinguish between the detective and the investigator; 'As I see it a detective may solve crimes purely on an intuitive basis, or by the employment of commonplace logic coupled with long experience and an understanding of human nature. These are the bases upon which crime is usually solved. The investigator on the other hand requires the ability to marshal facts, resources, procedures, hypotheses, priorities and information. He must, of course include amongst his resources his detective staff. From this, it follows that it will be hard to imagine a good investigator who is not a good detective. However, in the sense in which I use the word "many good detectives do not have the capacity to be good investigators"' (Kind 1987, p. 9). This quote provides the raison d'être for this chapter.

The ground-breaking study of Smith and Flanagan (2000), is still viewed today as a benchmark in relation to the qualities required of a SIO. They interviewed SIO's, and heads of CID to identify the competencies of SIO in terms of the skills, abilities and personality characteristics required of an investigator. Their detailed discussion of the requisite skills required for an SIO covered a diverse range of abilities from leadership and team building as the most frequently cited skill to organising the mechanics of the investigation and handling experts as the least cited skill (p. 21). They identified 22 different skills categories, which they were then able to group into three skill clusters: management skills, investigative ability and knowledge levels. They concluded that the effective SIO needs to have a combination of all three abilities across the investigative process.

The requirement for enhanced training of detectives in leadership and management to improve and professionalise the investigative function led to the introduction in 2005 of a vocational initiative referred to as Professionalising the Investigation Process (PIP). According to Neyroud and Disley (2007) the PIP seeks to improve investigation management and all other parts of the investigative process. The introduction of PIP acknowledged that criminal investigation required the development of a professional practice that investigators could be taught and examined against. As Stelfox (2007) has pointed out, police reforms to procedures usually occur after organisational failures to ensure that they do not happen again. However, instead of tackling procedural issues, the emphasis should be on improving the skills of the investigator, particularly within Homicide. The highly complex nature of modern twenty-first-century policing necessitates the shift from a traditionally based focus of the "omni-competent officer" to one with a more specialised role embodied within a professional practice (Stelfox 2007, p. 633).

IS PIP PROFESSIONALISING THE SIO ROLE?

Despite PIP and procedural improvements in the investigative sphere with the introduction of the MIRSAP, MIM and Core Investigative Doctrine[4] some researchers still question the efficacy of murder investigation. Brookman and Innes (2013, p. 294) from their study of homicide investigations suggest that pressures from senior officers to conclude an investigation can lead to shortcuts in procedure and process. They question if the new approaches to investigation are anymore effective than those of the past. James and Mills (2012, p. 139) report on the paucity of scholarly research and evaluation about the PIP process. Their small study took place within a single police force in England and was limited to six interviews, including that of the Chief Constable and Deputy Chief Constable. They found that interviewees regarded professionalisation of investigation as positive. However, concerns were still voiced regarding the influence of the "old" detective culture, the shortage of detectives, and whether the selection processes for those considering such a career are adequate. The fact that CID were overstretched in terms of resource allocation impacted upon their capability and capacity at a local level and in turn affected their work–life balance. This limited study only provides a snapshot of one force. Nevertheless, James and Mills (2012, p. 137) study highlights again that there has been no "significant independent research" on police training. This echoes the assessment of Tong (2009, p. 202) and Alys et al. (2013) who state that there is little publicly available to evaluate the strengths and weaknesses of the PIP. More significantly, Tong (2009), has also noted that despite the introduction of programmes to enhance police training and specifically detective training, the latter is still dominated by a "craft model of learning".

---

[4]The authors are aware that the Practice Advice on Core Investigation Doctrine is under review—personal communication from the College of Policing.

WHAT IS REQUIRED TO BE AN EFFECTIVE SIO
FOR A TWENTY-FIRST-CENTURY ROLE?

From our preliminary and ongoing analysis, in a very basic way, we see an effective SIO as an individual leader with good intellectual abilities who is able to demonstrate consistently that he or she can provide firm direction, supervision and guidance to their team, which may include external resources. Under significant and often enduring high pressure, they are able to quickly evaluate emerging and often complex information and shape the immediate investigative environment based on sound and transparent decision-making. In this way, they demonstrate "grip". If necessary, they are able to shift the investigative emphasis whilst maintaining control. This will include being receptive to different ideas, rather than focusing on one investigative theory to the detriment of others. This involves the flexibility of mind to remain objective when considering alternative explanations that may not initially align with their own and is underpinned by the requirement to work increasingly in a multidisciplinary team of other relevant investigative specialists. In that multidisciplinary context, ownership of "turf" is an outmoded and disadvantageous attitude for the complexity of today's challenges. At the same time, they will maintain independence of thought and not be unduly influenced by internal or external influences. It is a given that within the ambit of homicide investigation, an effective SIO will also have developed specialist theoretical and evidence-based knowledge about decision making and the interpretation of other sources of relevant complex information (including, for example, Forensic Pathology; Forensic Science; Forensic Psychology and Psychiatry) as it applies to types of homicide and homicide offenders.

Whilst experience is required, we suggest that it is investigative expertise that is essential to the task. Research differentiating experience and expertise has described experience as that which may be learnt from undertaking an activity or being involved in an event; alternatively, it may be acquired over a period of time. In a previous study, Alison et al. (2013) found that when aggravated by debilitating, time-dependent pressures, experience did not assist decision-makers in a simulated rape scenario. That which distinguishes experience from expertise, and the novice from the expert, is in the domain of deliberate practice. Expertise includes greater familiarity with aspects of a situation that assists in memory retrieval; enhanced images that capture the salient features of the domain; access to previous solutions and well-practiced component skills (Klein 1998). These elements also assist in distinguishing the expert from the novice (Ericsson 2006). Taken further, expertise requires extensive periods of education and deliberate practice or a combination of both. Mere passive acquisition is not enough (Fahsing and Ask 2013, 2016). In contrast to short courses and short-term deployments as investigators, we propose that the Police Service can only achieve the necessary remedy by committing to the development of the investigator role as a career specialism: Most areas of expertise require an estimate of either 10 years experience, or 10,000 hours of deliberate practice as a minimum (Ericsson et al. 2007).

Consequently, we believe that the complexity and scope of this investigative and evidential task, with its attendant responsibility and accountability, must be supported by training and career development pathways that are relevant to the SIO in twenty-first-century criminal investigation. Without demeaning the commitment and best efforts of many SIOs currently, our discussion and review indicate that the training of detectives and thereby SIO's continues to fall short of what is required for the current and future operational milieux.

Conclusion

Our review of the last half-century into the investigation of murder has drawn on a broad literature from the perspective of the practitioner and the researcher. Our awareness of more recent failures in critical analysis (Smith 2003, para 14.43); investigative decision making (Sentamu et al. 2002, paras 3.2.7–8); leadership (Sentamu et al. 2002); management (Macpherson 1999); direction (Flanagan 2004, para 5.4); and grip (Flanagan 2004, para 5.46) leads us to concur with Dame Janet Smith that, "some problems can be resolved only by the application of the minds of people with the necessary intelligence and experience" (Smith 2003, para 16.29). At the same time, we acknowledge that countless complex murder enquiries have been solved and accept that investigative success is an indicator of the qualities required to be an effective SIO. In that sense, we are also aware that our own review here is partial; we have focused more on failure than success. Unfortunately, it is usually investigative failures that end in unwanted publicity for the police force concerned.

Those investigations that have led to public reviews, invariably, have been followed by recommendations to reform aspects of the investigative process. Invariably, the Police Service has incorporated these recommendations in various forms of guidance to prevent further recurrences, however, the overall emphasis of such reforms has been to focus primarily on the procedure. Indeed, as an outward manifestation and acknowledgement of intent to continually improve and be effective, the Police Service introduced the PIP process as way of stating that the lessons of the public inquiries had been learnt. However, to our knowledge, the PIP process has not yet been evaluated to establish if it is actually achieving what it was intended to do.

We acknowledge the efforts that have been made to remedy the failings identified by public reviews. Nevertheless, we argue that in addition to improvements in procedure, the Police Service should acknowledge the plain fact that the basic premise of a professional organisation lies in having an appropriate corpus of professional knowledge. The attainment of that corpus of knowledge as a necessary foundation for the discipline and practice of investigation requires a radical change to the current training and development of investigators. In the first instance, the investigative function should be recognised as sufficiently distinct from mainstream policing and therefore deservedly requiring "a separate professional practice" Stelfox (2007, p. 629) and specialisation (West 2001).

The development of SIO expertise should also be recognised as requiring the summation of relevant theoretical and conceptual domain knowledge, enhanced decision-making skills and the accumulation of investigative experience that allows ready access to conceptual and practical models for action. An understanding of how other disciplines can assist the investigative process requires more than a superficial familiarity with their methods and procedures. Thus, forensic science, forensic pathology, behavioural science and the science of evidence (Dawid et al. 2011) should be considered at least as basic components of a necessary core curriculum with associated education in leadership, management, ethics, criminal law and legal procedures (West 2001). These requirements imply commitment to continuing academic education, testing by formal examination and continuing vocational training, all mediated by the reality of immersion in live enquiries. The emphasis should be on the acquisition of critical thinking and complex problem-solving skills, with the acceptance that in the face of increasing complexity, successful and cost-effective investigations will require the collaboration of highly able personnel from a range of investigative backgrounds. The time for piece-meal reform of the investigative process has passed. Even the most cursory comparison of the training and development that underpins the role of other similar professional groups, signals that the twenty-first-century SIO and the public he or she protects, require a professional role founded on a professional education. The scale of the responsibility and accountability of the SIO role demands that their training and development should be of the highest standard to ensure the best possible service in undertaking what can prove to be one of the most demanding and challenging of all crimes, the investigation of murder.

REFERENCES

ACPO. (2005a). *Guidance on Major Incident Room Standardised Administrative Procedures (MIRSAP)*. Wyboston: NPIA.

ACPO. (2005b). *Practice Advice on Core Investigative Doctrine*. Wyboston: NPIA.

ACPO. (2006). *Murder Investigation Manual*. Wyboston: NPIA.

Adhami, E., & Browne, D. P. (1996). *Major Crime Enquiries: Improving Expert Support for Detectives* (Home Office Police Research Group Special Interest Series Paper 9). London: Home Office.

Alison, L., Doran, B., Long, M., Power, N., & Humphrey, A. (2013). The Effects of Subjective Time Pressures and Individual Differences on Hypotheses Generation and Action Prioritisation in Police Investigations. *Journal of Experimental Psychology: Applied, 19*(1), 83–93. https://doi.org/10.1037/a0032148.

Alys, L., Massey, K., & Tong, S. (2013). Investigative Decision Making: Missing People and Sexual Offences, Crossroads to an Uncertain Future. *Journal of Investigative Psychology and Offender Profiling, 10*(2), 140–154.

Baron, J. (2008). *Thinking and Deciding*. Cambridge: Cambridge University Press.

Brookman, F. (2005). *Understanding Homicide*. London: Sage.

Brookman, F., & Innes, M. (2013). The Problem of Success: What Is a 'Good' Homicide Investigation? *Policing & Society, 23*(3), 292–310. https://doi.org/10.1080/10439463.2013.771538.

Bruhns, J. (1982). Police and Homicides. In L. Danto, J. Bruhns, & A. H. Kutscher (Eds.), *The Human Side of Homicide*. New York: Columbia University Press.

Bryant, R. P. (2009) Theories of Investigation. In S. Tong, R. P. Bryant, & M. Horvath (Eds.), *Understanding Criminal Investigation* (pp. 13–35). Hoboken, NJ: Wiley.

Byford, L. (1981). *The Yorkshire Ripper Case: Review of the Police Investigation of the Case by Lawrence Byford, Esq., CBE., QPM., Her Majesty's Inspector of Constabulary.* London: HMSO.

Carson, D. (2007). Models of Investigation. In T. Newburn, T. Williamson, & A. Wright (Eds.), *Handbook of Criminal Investigations* (pp. 407–425). London: Willan.

Carson, D. (2009). Detecting, Developing and Disseminating Detectives' "Creative" Skills. *Policing and Society, 19*(3), 216–225. https://doi.org/10.1080/10439460902871322.

Carson, D. (2013). Investigations: What Could, and Should, Be Taught. *The Police Journal, 86,* 249–275. https://doi.org/10.1350/pojo.2013.86.3.628.

Cook, T., & Tattersall, A. (2016). *Senior Investigating Officers' Handbook* (4th ed.). Oxford: Oxford University Press.

Dawid, P., Twining, W., & Vasilaki, M. (Eds.). (2011). Evidence, Inference and Enquiry. In *Proceedings of the British Academy 171.* Oxford: Oxford University Press.

Dean, G., Fahsing, I. A., & Gottschalk, P. (2006). Profiling Police Investigative Thinking: A Study of Police Officers in Norway. *International Journal of the Sociology of Law* [e-journal], *34*(4), 221–228. https://doi.org/10.1016/j.ijsl.2006.09.002.

du Rose, J. (1971). *Murder Was My Business.* London: W. H. Allen.

Ericsson, K. A. (2006). An Introduction to the Cambridge Handbook of Expertise and Expert Performance: Its Development, Organisation and Content. In K. A. Ericsson, N. Charness, P. Feltovich, & R. Hoffman (Eds.), *The Cambridge Handbook of Expertise and Expert Performance* (pp. 3–21). New York, NY: Cambridge University Press.

Ericsson, K. A., Prietula, M. J., & Cokely, E. T. (2007). The Making of an Expert. *Harvard Business Review, 85*(7–8), 114–121.

Fahsing, I., & Ask, K. (2013). Decision Making and Decisional Tipping Points in Homicide Investigations: An Interview Study of British and Norwegian Detectives. *Journal of Investigative Psychology and Offender Profiling, 10,* 155–165. https://doi.org/10.1002/jip.1384.

Fahsing, I., & Ask, K. (2016). The Making of an Expert Detective: The Role of Experience in English and Norwegian Police Officer's Investigative Decision Making. *Psychology Crime & Law, 22*(3), 203–223. https://doi.org/10.1080/1068316x.2015.1077249.

Flanagan, Sir R. (2004). *A Report on the Investigation by Cambridgeshire Constabulary into the Murder of Jessica Chapman and Holly Wells at Soham on 4 August 2002: Summary of Conclusions and Recommendations.* London: HMIC.

Forbes, I. (1973). *Squad Man.* London: W. H. Allen.

HMIC. (2017). *PEEL: Police Effectiveness: A National Overview.* London: HMIC.

Hobbs, D. (1988). *Doing the Business: Entrepreneurship, Detectives's and the Working Class in the East End of London*. Oxford: Oxford University Press.

Innes, M. (2002a). Organisational Communication and the Symbolic Construction of Police Murder Investigations. *British Journal of Sociology*, *53*(1), 67–87. https://doi.org/10.1080/00071310120109339.

Innes, M. (2002b). The 'Process Structures' of Police Homicide Investigations. *The British Journal of Criminology, 42*, 669–688.

Innes, M. (2003). *Investigating Murder: Detective Work and the Police Response to Criminal Homicide*. Oxford: Oxford University Press.

Innes, M. (2007). Investigation Order and Major Crime Inquiries. In T. Newburn, T. Williamson, & A. Wright (Eds.), *Handbook of Criminal Investigations* (pp. 255–277). London: Willan.

Irving, B., & Dunnighan, C. (1993). *Human Factors in the Quality Control of CID Investigations*. London: HMSO.

Irving, B., & McKenzie, I. (1993). A Brief Review of Relevant Police Training. In *The Royal Commission on Criminal Justice: Human Factors in the Quality Control of CID Investigations* (pp. 77–100). Research Study No 21. London: HMSO.

James, A., & Mills, M. (2012). Does ACPO Know Best: To What Extent May the PIP Programme Provide a Template for the Professionalising of Policing? *The Police Journal: Theory, Practice and Principles, 85*(2), 133–149. https://doi.org/10.1350/pojo.2012.85.2.587.

Kassin, S. M. (2012). Why Confessions Trump Innocence. *American Psychological Association, 67*(6), 431–445. https://doi.org/10.1037/a0028212.

Kind, S. (1987). *The Scientific Investigation of Crime*. Manchester, UK: Forensic Science Services Limited.

Klein, G. (1998). *Sources of Power: How People Make Decisions*. Cambridge: MIT Press.

Leo, R. A. (2008). *Police Interrogation and American Justice*. Cambridge, MA: Harvard University Press.

Macpherson, Sir W. M. (1999). *The Stephen Lawrence Inquiry*. London: HMSO.

Maguire, M. (2008). Criminal Investigation and Crime Control. In T. Newburn (Ed.), *Handbook of Policing* (pp. 430–464). London. Willan.

Mark, Sir, R. (1978). *In the Office of Constable*. London: William Collins & Sons Ltd.

Neyroud, P., & Disley, E. (2007). The Management, Supervision and Oversight of Criminal Investigations. In T. Newburn, T. Williamson, & A. Wright (Eds.), *Handbook of Criminal Investigation* (pp. 549–572). London: Willan.

Oughton, F. (1971). *Murder Investigation*. London: Elek Books Limited.

Powis, D. (1977). *The Signs of Crime: A Field Manual for Police*. London: McGraw-Hill.

Riener, R. (2010). *The Politics of the Police* (4th ed.). Oxford: Oxford University Press.

Roycroft, M., Brown, J., & Innes, M. (2007). Reform by Crisis: The Murder of Stephen Lawrence and Socio-Historical Analysis of Developments in the Conduct of Major Crime Investigations. In M. Rowe (Ed.), *Policing Beyond MacPherson: Issues in Policing, Race and Society* (pp. 148–164). Cullompton, Devon: Willan.

Runciman, Viscount of Doxford. (1993). *The Royal Commission on Criminal Justice*. London. HMSO (Cm 2263).

Savage, S. P., & Milne, B. (2007). Miscarriages of Justice. In T. Newburn, T. Williamson, & A. Wright (Eds.), *Handbook of Criminal Investigation* (pp. 610–628). London: Willan.

Schon, D. A. (1983). *The Reflective Practitioner*. New York, NY: Basic Books.

Sentamu, Rt Revd. J., Blakey, D., & Nove, P. (2002). *The Damilola Taylor Murder Investigation Review: The Report of the Oversight Panel*. Presented to Sir John Stevens QPM DL Commissioner of the Metropolis, December 2002.

Simon, D. (2012). *In Doubt: The Psychology of the Criminal Justice System*. Cambridge, MA: Harvard University Press.

Smith, D. J. (2003). *The Shipman Inquiry Second Report: The Police Investigation of March 1998*. London. HMSO.

Smith, N., & Flanagan, C. (2000). *The Effective Detective: Identifying the Skills of an Effective SIO* (Police Research Series Paper No. 122). London: Home Office.

Stead, P. J. (1977). Preface. In D. Powis (Ed.), *The Signs of Crime: A Field Manual for Police*. London: McGraw-Hill.

Stelfox, P. (2007). Professionalising Criminal Investigation. In T. Newburn, T. Williamson, & A. Wright (Eds.), *Handbook of Criminal Investigations* (pp. 628–651). London: Willan.

Stelfox, P. (2009). *Criminal Investigation: An Introduction to Principles and Practice*. Devon: Willan.

Stelfox, P., & Pease, K. (2005). Cognition and Detection: Reluctant Bedfellows? In N. J. Smith & N. Tilley (Eds.), *Crime Science: New Approaches to Preventing and Detecting Crime* (pp. 191–207). Cullopmton, Devon: Willan.

Tate, T., & Wyre, R. (1992). *Murder Squad*. London: Methuen.

Tong, S. (2009). Professionalising Investigation. In S. Tong, R. P. Bryant, & M. Horvath (Eds.), *Understanding Criminal Investigation* (pp. 197–214). Hoboken, NJ: Wiley.

Tong, S., Bryant, R. P., & Horvath, M. (2009). *Understanding Criminal Investigation*. Hoboken, NJ: Wiley.

West, A. (2001). A Proposal for an Investigative Science Course: Any Takers? *Police Research and Management, 5*, 13–22.

West, A., & Alison, L. (2005). Conclusions: Personal Reflections on the Last Decade. In L. Alison (Ed.), *The Forensic Psychologists Casebook: Psychological Profiling and Criminal Investigation* (pp. 380–392). Cullompton, Devon: Willan.

CHAPTER 8

The Retrospective Detective: Cognitive Bias and the Cold Case Investigation

Jason Roach

Abstract Much of the available research on police decision-making in criminal investigations tends to focus on the detrimental effects of cognitive bias in live/current homicide investigations, and not on how it might have a negative influence on investigative decision-making in cold case homicides. This arguably indicates the existence of a common assumption that, live or cold, criminal investigations require the same decision-making and so are vulnerable to the same bias and in the same ways. This chapter suggests that the very term 'cold case' is likely to have a different psychological bias effect on investigators of cold cases and to pose potentially a far stronger negative influence on the decisions that are made in cold

A shorter version of this chapter was published as Roach, J. (2017). The Retrospective Detective. Cognitive Bias and the Cold Case Homicide Investigator. *Papers from the British Criminology Conference. Vol. 17.* ISSN 1759-0043. Found at: http://www.britsoccrim.org/wp-content/uploads/2017/12/The-Retrospective-Detective.pdf.

J. Roach (✉)
University of Huddersfield, Huddersfield, UK
e-mail: j.roach@hud.ac.uk

© The Author(s) 2019
M. Roycroft and J. Roach (eds.),
Decision Making in Police Enquiries and Critical Incidents,
https://doi.org/10.1057/978-1-349-95847-4_8

as opposed to live cases. The idea that cold cases necessitate a different 'investigative mindset' to live cases is posited here, along with the suggestion that investigator confidence is likely to be undermined by an inherent framing effect which comes into play when people are told that they are to investigate a cold case, that does not with live cases. Also discussed are the implications of having to make decisions based on the result of numerous previous decisions made by prior police investigators, might have on cold-case investigators. This may in turn serve to increase the likelihood of confirmation bias when investigators review cold cases as they make decisions within a far more pessimistic frame than they do for live cases. The chapter ends with a tentative research agenda for increasing our understanding of decision-making processes in cold case homicide investigations.

Keywords 'Omincompetent detective' · Investigative decision-making · Cognitive bias and the homicide investigator · Cold case homicide investigations

INTRODUCTION

> The objective of reviewing previously undetected homicide cases is to identify those that have potential for re-investigation in order to catch the person responsible. This will not always be possible but the key message from the police to the families and the perpetrators must be "we still care" and "murder investigations are never closed. (Gaynor 2002, p. iv.)

Some crimes are unsolvable. Mercifully, most are not. The purpose of this chapter is not to question the balance of priority police should give to unsolved crimes committed in the distant past, but to suggest that investigators need to be made aware of the likely different factors and influences on their thinking and decision-making when investigating 'cold' as opposed to 'live' (or current) cases. Differences that could influence the decisions they make and the conclusions that they draw. Put simply, a case is made in the present chapter that undetected 'cold' case homicides warrant a slightly different, but potentially significant, investigative mindset, to that encouraged for example in the Murder Investigation Manual (MIM). The MIM was developed after all for 'all homicide investigations, based on the assumption that the guidance should be the same regardless of whether the investigation is 'live' or 'cold'. If this thinking is extrapolated, then another likely assumption attached to this more general assumption is that in both types of investigation, investigators are at the same risk of cognitive bias, from the same types and to the same degree. This chapter challenges these 'assumptions' by suggesting that investigators are at risk of cognitive bias in different ways in cold cases compared with live, particularly the probable framing effect inherent in use of the term 'cold case' itself, which is likely to have a negative effect on the confidence of investigators and subsequently on how they then approach, conduct and make decisions in a cold case investigation.

This chapter serves as no more than a thought provoker to encourage thinking about the thinking involved in cold case investigations, with no new empirical evidence offered.[1] In my partial defence, however, what is presented here is an argument that cold and live case investigations necessitate different thinking and decision-making, based upon an appreciation of the research literature on human decision-making, cognitive bias and error, and criminal investigation, coupled with a decade (or more) of observing detectives making decisions in criminal investigations. As a final word in my defence (or excuse) for failing to present any new empirical evidence with which to support my suggestions, (although I do encourage your participation in a thought experiment a little later on) a tentative research agenda is offered at the end of the chapter in the hope of encouraging others to explore how investigators make decisions in cold case investigations (as opposed to live ones). First, and to quote Julie Andrews, 'let's start at the very beginning', with a general look at homicide investigation and how investigative decision-making has evolved in the UK.

In the UK at least, the concept of the detective as a specialist role requiring specific knowledge, skills, experience and resources (Atkin and Roach 2015) has evolved over time as part of a wider move away from the traditional 'omnicompetent' view of the police officer, who is adept at any aspect of policing with equal aplomb (Stelfox 2008). Modern-day detectives, despite often being considered specialised (e.g. at investigating

---

[1] Thank you to one of my colleagues (Dr. Wright) for pointing out that unless I am upfront about this early in chapter, then some readers may become disappointed waiting for a train that never comes. Hopefully any potential disappointment has now been avoided.

homicide) are also expected to be generalists who can investigate all manner of serious crimes, including rape and robbery (Roach and Pease 2014). Indeed, very few outside of the large, metropolitan forces/ services will be tasked solely with investigating homicide. Even amongst homicide investigations, the forensic contexts can be diverse, ranging from a gangland killing to the murder of a husband by his wife—homicide investigations can be very different. Although criminal investigation is seen as requiring different skills and knowledge sets to those of more mainstream policing, an 'omnicompetent' view of the detective is arguably still propagated by the fact that the same officers investigate all types of homicide, despite recent questioning that this is the best approach when significant differences in investigative thinking and processes in 'live', and 'cold cases 'are present (Atkin and Roach 2015).

This chapter focuses on one aspect of the 'omnicompetent detective' assumption, whereby it is assumed that criminal investigators need to possess the same skill set, knowledge base and professional experience, irrespective of whether the case being investigated is a current (i.e. live), historic or 'cold' case homicide. Although the research literature on investigative decision-making in homicide investigations has grown in recent years with examples of how different types of cognitive bias, such as *'tunnel vision'* (e.g. Rossmo 2009; McLean and Roach 2011), *confirmation bias* (e.g. Rossmo 2009; Roach and Pease 2014) and the *'representativeness heuristic'* (e.g. Rossmo 2009; McLean and Roach 2011; Roach and Pease 2014) can and do negatively influence criminal investigations, two assumptions appear still to prevail, with the second being dependent on the first

1. The same types of investigative decision are made irrespective of whether an investigation is live, historic or cold, and if so
2. Exactly the same types and contexts for cognitive bias exist that pose the same risks to both live and cold homicide investigations.

By focusing specifically on this as yet neglected area of decision-making in cold case investigations, this chapter challenges the assumption that live and cold homicide investigations have the same investigative decision-making requirements and therefore carry the same potential for the same cognitive bias, and in equal measure. We begin by looking briefly at the wider context of human decision-making before moving to the investigative context more specifically.

HUMAN DECISION-MAKING
(AND POLICE INVESTIGATORS ARE HUMAN, RIGHT!)

Criminal investigators are human beings. As such their investigative decision-making relies on the same cognitive systems and processes as the decision-making used in other (non-forensic) environments and contexts, honed and selected as useful over evolutionary timescales. As the evolutionary underpinnings of decision-making are dealt masterfully by Robin Bryant in Chapter Four, it suffices to say here that psychologists have identified two broad decision-making processes (although admittedly considered an over-simplistic model by some). The first, *System 1*, operates quickly, automatically, effortlessly, associatively and is often emotionally charged (Stanovich and West 2000; Kahneman 2003, 2011) and represents what many of us would consider to be 'intuition' or 'habit'. By contrast, *System 2* processing is slower, more effortful, controlled, serial and is 'relatively flexible and potentially rule-bound' (Kahneman 2003, 2011). System 2 processing represents what many of us would consider to be 'rational thought' or our ability to think more deeply about things and consider our actions before we act. Out of necessity (e.g. not enough hours in the day) or laziness, of course many of the decisions that we make during the course of a day will rely mainly on only System 1 thinking, that is these decisions are intuitive and do not consciously employ formal types of reasoning. This holds important implications for understanding wider investigative decision-making and for decision-making in cold case investigations (particularly homicide). Why?

As noted above, one of the defining properties of System 1, intuitive thought, is that it comes automatically and relies on '*accessibility*' (Tory Higgins 1996). Accessibility for example, can be the mention of a familiar object (such as a tree) or social category (such as 'traveller') and a wealth of associated information related to the category stereotype comes to mind. The writer is reminded of an occasion when, on asking several officers with over twenty years' police service, 'who commits most of the acquisitive crime on your patch?', all three immediately replied, 'those from the traveller community'. When challenged to qualify their answers, the three were found to be from different forces (one had Leeds city centre as his patch), and all admitted that the last couple of arrests he had made had been individuals from the traveller community. On reflection, all three agreed that perhaps their reply had been greatly influenced by recent events (recency effect) and was perhaps subject to exaggeration.[2] Psychologists refer to this type of System 1 thinking as schema theory, whereby for example, on mention of the word 'tree', associated information (schemas) is brought to mind, such as 'branch', 'acorns', 'conkers', 'leaves' and 'huggers'.

The more intuitive reader will see where this is going. What I posit here is that on mention of the word 'cold- case investigation', a specific schema or stream of associated information will be triggered in the System 1 thinking of our criminal investigator which is likely to have a great influence on how she perceives any cold case homicide, or at least where her thinking about a cold case is likely to begin. Indeed, as previously suggested, when System 1 thinking is solely engaged then the subsequent decision-making process is vulnerable to different cognitive biases. It is suggested here that cold case homicide investigators are perhaps more vulnerable to several types of cognitive bias in different ways to those investigating live homicide cases. Such potentially different bias effects on investigator decision-making are not currently identified in the investigative guidance available to UK police (e.g. MIM). A brief discussion of the guidance available to police investigators in England and Wales now follows, with the remainder of the chapter then dedicated to what and how specific cognitive bias can influence cold case decision-making both in form and intensity.

Procedural Guidance and the Criminal Investigator

...the MIM is a comprehensive set of guidelines to assist the SIO in the conduct of the investigation itself. (Fox 2007, p. 139)

With regard to the conduct of criminal investigations, police in England and Wales are guided both generically by *The Core Investigative Doctrine* (CID) and *Major Incident Room Standard Administrative Procedures* (MIRSAP).[3] These can be considered generic in the sense that they can

---

[2] Interestingly when I asked if they often recovered the items stolen in the burglaries that they were investigating, all three said that they did not usually, but did find some from other burglaries, so always a 'result'!

[3] Theses and guidance on specific forms of homicide (e.g. child) are grouped together by the College of Policing under Authorised Professional Practice and can be found at https://www.app.college.police.uk/app-content/major-investigation-and-public-protection/homicide/? (Accessed on the 12 December 2016).

be applied to a host of different types of criminal investigation, and also more specifically, for example when investigating homicide then the MIM is pertinent. It is not my intention to criticise such professional guidance, indeed there is much to commend in trying to make criminal investigative practice and procedures more systematic and consistent and in providing valuable support to neophyte investigators. These publications must not be overly-prescriptive as homicide is committed in a wide array of different contexts and scenarios, for example, gangland killings, the killing of a child by its step-parent or killing by reckless driving. Moreover, murders do not occur in the same circumstances and contexts so even if a definitive guide to investigating all murders was desired it would be unachievable, opting instead to provide an outline of the necessary procedural requirements and processes (including evidential standards) for those conducting criminal investigations to consult and follow. Such guidance also provides a suitable benchmark by which individual investigations can be judged or reviewed, particularly those considered not to have reached a satisfactory conclusion (e.g. the identification and successful prosecution of a suspect). Such investigative cul-de-sacs commonly represent our 'cold- cases'. With this backdrop, two questions are begged:

1. Is the thinking and decision-making required in all types of homicide investigation the same and if so does this matter? If not, and it does matter, then
2. Which significant differences exist in the investigation of live, historic and 'cold' case homicide investigations, and are these subject to different types and degrees of cognitive bias?

Decision-Making, Cognitive Bias and the Homicide Investigator

The success of a criminal investigation (i.e. where a suspect is successfully identified, charged and convicted) largely depends on the correct decision-making of the investigator (Fahsing and Ask 2013). We do not, however, live in a world that always facilitates such correct or optimal decision-making. Optimal decision-making is often influenced by the pressures of the job, such as limited time and the competition for resources. Perhaps unsurprisingly, as Ivar Fahsing suggested in a previous chapter, investigator objectivity has consistently been shown often to be debilitated (e.g. Ask and Granhag 2007; Fahsing and Ask 2013) and has led to numerous examples of miscarriages of justice (see e.g. Rossmo 2009 for a fuller discussion replete with excellent examples).

Gollwitzer (1990) suggests that much human decision-making and consequently behaviour is 'goal directed'. That is, we humans make decisions with specific goals in mind and there is little doubt that criminal investigators are any less human in this respect. Building on Gollwitzer and colleagues early work (Gollwitzer et al. 1990) Fahsing and Ask (2013) tested the cognitive performance of criminal investigators decision-making, across different stages of goal-directed behaviour, and found that when investigators were in the 'deliberative mindset', they were more open-minded and generated a greater number of hypotheses (e.g. about what might have happened and why), than when they adopted a more closed and narrow 'implemental mindset' (see Fahsing's chapter earlier in this book for a fuller account).

The first question to ask when looking at cognitive bias in cold case investigations is whether these cases are more likely to encourage an implemental rather than deliberative mindset in the investigator. The short answer suggested here is yes. Next follow some suggestions (in no particular order) for how and why this is likely to be more the case for investigative thinking and decision-making in cold cases, compared with that of live homicide investigation. Let us begin with the common perceptions of the prefix 'live', 'historic' and 'cold', when placed in front of 'homicide'.

1. *Live, historic and cold homicide investigation. Substantively or semantically different?*

The logical place to start is with what live, historic, and cold homicide cases are considered to actually mean, although these are not mutually exclusive or invariant over time. In fact, this is part of my argument that investigators want to place the homicide into one of these three categories and keep them there as this influences the mindset employed. There are, by the way, no fixed, concrete definitions of the three types of case available, so I am going to go out on a limb and suggest how each is different to the other two. Referred to commonly as a *Live* homicide (although seeming an oxymoron on first hearing) this represents a current or recent case being investigated, whereby *cold* refers (arguably unsympathetically) to those cases where the investigation is yet to yield a satisfactory conclusion (i.e. the killer has not been prosecuted or more commonly is yet to be identified). Although these often appear as two discrete categories created for investigative purposes, one must not forget that all cold homicides began as live cases and some cold cases become live again should, for example, a new witness come forward or new forensic evidence come to light. Use of the term *historic* homicides remains less defined, but generally is taken to represent cases where suspects are identified after a significant period of time, for example, convicted killer Peter Tobin, where the gardens of his previous homes were searched for further victims after he was identified to be a serial murderer. Admittedly, more recently 'historic' has become a category more synonymous with past 'child sexual exploitation' (Roach 2016) but again where allegations of historic child abuse are investigated against a known suspect, and will not be focussed upon here as much as 'live' and 'cold' homicide cases.

So is deciding whether a homicide is live, historic or cold, of any real importance to an investigator or are we just playing semantics? The short answer is again yes, it is important. First, it is likely to affect the investigator's initial level of confidence with regard to achieving a satisfactory investigative outcome. Figure 8.1 shows a hypothetical chart of the flow of investigator confidence across all three different categories of homicide investigation.

Let us hypothesise further that all investigators begin live homicide investigations with the belief that they all assume that they will get a satisfactory result, so investigator confidence in all live investigations should be highest initially. Given that murder investigation clearance rate in the England and Wales stands at about 92% of all cases per year, then it can be argued that such confidence is well founded. For those beginning an investigation of historic homicide, initial confidence is not likely to be as high, but if they are investigating allegations against a likely suspect, it should be reasonably high. As Davis et al. (2014) point out, in the USA, although there is no 'universally accepted metric for when a case becomes cold', one year is seen by many to be the boundary between live and cold cases in homicide. In the UK, this is arguably a bit of throwback to the old days of the 'year and a day' rule in English law for murder. More importantly, it perhaps reflects the damaging effects of assumptions in the police service about how criminal behaviour and investigative processes and procedures are 'naturally' seasonal, with all investigative loose ends tied-up within the calendar months and seasons

- **Live homicide investigations**
- **Historic homicide investigations**
- **Cold case homicide investigations**

Fig. 8.1 Investigator confidence in different types of homicide investigation

of the year, when of course in reality many are not. For those embarking on this type of homicide case, the fact that it is referred to as 'cold' means that it will be considered the most difficult type to solve with possibly many investigators likely to have tried but to no avail in the past. Somewhat unsurprisingly then, confidence in the likelihood that they will get a result is likely to be much lower for these cases.

Some of the most immediate and obvious investigative differences between live and cold homicide cases are presented in Table 8.1.

As Table 8.1 suggests, the level of control that police investigators (e.g. SIOs) have over the conducing of live homicide cases appears to be much greater than for that of cold cases, primarily because it appears, at face value at least, that the cold case investigator has little more to work with beyond that provided by previous investigators and their investigations. She cannot turn back the clock and begin the investigation afresh as the original investigator has. She is not afforded that luxury, especially when her decisions are based on those made by her predecessors. Compared with live and historic homicide investigations, the cold case investigator's lot does not seem a happy one with the likelihood of a successful detection often looking slim or impossible.

Framing is 'the passive acceptance of the formulation given' (Kahneman 2003, p. 1450). That is, by definition, the frame for cold case homicides is that they are difficult if not impossible to solve, unless, for example, there has been a recent breakthrough in forensic science (as it was with DNA evidence advancement ten years or so ago) or new criminal intelligence, such as information from a known criminal. If not, then the psychological effect on an officer(s) charged with investigating a cold case is likely to be one of pessimism, with consequently the common psychological frame likely to be adopted by detectives for cold cases a far more negative one when compared with that for live and historic investigations. Put simply, the psychological frame for cold cases appears to be one of narrow investigative control with the investigative direction

Table 8.1 Investigative differences in live and cold homicide investigations

Live cases	Cold cases
Fresh	Previously investigated (possibly many times)
Real time	Long interval in time since the crime
High optimism	Low optimism
Greater chance of reliable witnesses	Less chance of reliable witnesses
Good chance of forensic evidence	Less chance of more forensic evidence
Control over gathering and storing of evidence	Little control over storing of past evidence
Greater utility of public appeals	Little utility in public appeals
Pressure is immediate	Pressure is less but constant
Offender likely to be alive	Fair chance offender is deceased

contingent on decisions made in previous investigations. The latter being a point that we shall revisit a little later.

A next obvious question is whether investigators are likely to be equally pessimistic about all cold cases that they are asked to investigate? Is the frame for all cold case homicides likely to be equally narrow? If so, then it is likely to have the same effect on investigators at the initial point of case allocation, irrespective of the cold case in question (i.e. a cold case is a cold case)? For example, is an investigator assigned to a cold case homicide likely to perceive it (or even approach it) in the same way as they would one that involves a previous gross miscarriage of justice, as in the murder of Lesley Molseed, where the innocent, Stefan Kiszko, was imprisoned for sixteen years until eventually being found not guilty by the Supreme Court (Roach and Pease 2014). A brief discussion of 'solvability criteria' and how this might also influence investigator confidence and decision-making in cold case homicides is presented next.

2. Solvability criteria and investigator confidence in homicide investigations

Dugan et al. (1999) found that although in the 1960s the vast majority of victims of homicide knew their killers, by 1992 in the USA, this had dropped to 53%, making homicide cases harder to solve. The knock-on effect on clear-up rates was negative with a rise in the percentage becoming undetected, cold cases, particularly for 'stranger on stranger' murders often the most difficult to detect, particularly when a firearm has been used (Ousey and Lee 2009) and where the homicide occurs in a high-crime rate area (Borg and Parker 2001). Roach (2012) in a study of two famous 'long interval detections' (where the homicide was solved decades after the crime by a DNA hit which identified the killer) found that detection had been severely hindered as both offenders had moved away from the area of the crime soon after the murder.

In regard to cold case investigations, funded by the UK Home Office, *Operation Stealth* saw Government funding made available for numerous cold cases where DNA had been recovered from the scene or from the victim, and although effective, it only saw the targeting of the low-hanging fruit with regard to the solving of cold cases, with unfortunately a significant number of cold case homicides still remaining. For example, there are currently 50 undetected (i.e. cold) homicide cases going back since 1976, in the County of West Yorkshire in the UK, which has a general population of several million people.

So what do we know generally about the solvability of cold case homicide, or at least police perceptions of it? The short answer is not a lot. Davis et al. (2014) from a study of 189 solved and unsolved cases in Washington, DC, found that new information from witnesses or information from new witnesses (often criminal informants) was cited as the most common reason for case clear up. For cold cases specifically; crime context, initial investigation results, the basis for opening a cold case and cold case investigator action, were found to be the factors which best predicted whether a case would be solved. Perhaps surprisingly it was not forensic evidence. For police in England and Wales, the Association of Chief Police Officers (Now the National Police Chiefs' Council) has produced a 'Risk Assessment Matrix' for helping individual forces determine the solvability of cold cases, but application of the matrix is not compulsory and many forces have developed their own ways of prioritising cold cases according to their own solvability criteria (Marshall 2012, p. 214).

So how is the perceived solvability of a case likely to influence the psychology and decision-making of the cold case homicide investigator? This is where we turn next, starting with a return to the importance of the interval of time on perceptions of a crime.

3. *Cognitive bias, time and the investigation of crime*

Although admittedly only hypothesised here, one likely framing influence on cold case investigators' decision-making is how confident they are of being able to get a satisfactory outcome (e.g. identifying the offender) when there has been a significant time interval between the original crime and when an investigator is asked to revive the case. That is, the time since a crime has occurred is likely to impact on investigator confidence in achieving a successful outcome. Box 8.1, although hypothetical at this point, suggests a likely relationship between investigator confidence and the length of time a homicide remains undetected, although admittedly, in reality the relationship between time and confidence is likely to be far less linear.

Box 8.1 Investigator confidence and the passing of time since a homicide (% confident that a successful outcome will be achieved)*

Day 1—confidence starts high (e.g. 95%).
Day 7—with no firm lead to a suspect it drops (e.g. now at 80%)
Day 14—with no leads to a suspect(s) it drops again (e.g. now at 70%).
Day 28—with still no suspect leads it falls further (e.g. now at 50%).
3 months (undetected)—confidence is lowered (e.g. now at 40%).
6 months (undetected)—confidence is lowered (e.g. now at 30%).
1 year (undetected)—confidence is lowered (now at 25%).
2 years (undetected)—confidence is next to nothing (e.g. 5–10%).
10 years (undetected)—confidence of success has reached an all-time low (e.g. 5% or less).
20 years (undetected)—confidence is at 0%

*The confidence percentages given are merely illustrative.

Although merely illustrative, the point being made is that investigator (and police force) confidence in achieving a successful outcome is likely to decrease as time passes, with the cold case investigator, for example likely to be far less confident of achieving a satisfactory outcome after a two-year interval since the original crime (i.e. a detection) than the investigator of the same crime six months after it occurred. Unless of course there is a major shift in its perceived solvability, when for example a significant witness comes forward, the discovery of new forensic evidence (e.g. DNA) or the offender confesses.

The reader may feel justified at this point in thinking that the effect of time on investigator confidence is obvious and irrelevant, and has nothing to do with the investigative decision-making at all, as all homicide investigations must be carried out in the same way irrespective of whether they are live or cold. As stated earlier, the purpose of this chapter is merely to question this assumption and suggest that further research is warranted. The hypothesis posited is that cold case investigations demand a slightly different investigative mindset because they are in many different ways to live investigations, which need to be acknowledged. The effect of elapsed time is not the only important influence of potential bias here on investigator (and force) confidence in cold case homicide investigations. Please take a little time to engage in the brief thought experiment presented in Box 8.2.

Box 8.2 Framing effects and investigator confidence

Imagine that you are a police investigator given the cold case homicide of a young woman killed two years ago.

1. Based on this information how confident do you think that you would be able to solve this case?
2. You quickly discover a new potential witness but no new forensic evidence. Now how confident do you think that you would be able to solve this case?
3. Upon reading the case files you see that a number of great detectives have worked on this case in the past. Now how confident do you think that you would be able to solve this case?
4. A number of live homicide cases come in at the same time with which you must be involved and are also told that few resources are available to you for this cold case investigation. Now how confident do you think that you would be able to solve this case?

How confident are you now that you can progress this investigation in any way?

The rudimentary and unsophisticated point of Box 8.2 is to demonstrate simply how investigator confidence might be easily influenced by the addition of new information, for example discovering a new witness is more likely to increase confidence, where unless you are a total egotist, realising that some great detectives have tried to solve the case in the past is more likely to reduce it. Investigator confidence, like the mortgage rate can go up as well as down as the context and frame change. The point being that how an investigator perceives a cold case can be influenced by a host of different variables, such as whether the case was previously investigated by a renowned detective, which in turn can affect their level of confidence in achieving a successful outcome. Put bluntly, if you believe a case to be unsolvable before you've actually looked at it, then it most certainly is. That is, 'you've been framed' and another victim of confirmation bias.

CONFIRMATION BIAS AND THE COLD CASE HOMICIDE INVESTIGATION

Another form of cognitive bias, and arguably the most researched, is confirmation bias (or verification bias if you are American) whereby people tend to seek information that supports an existing belief over that which refutes or challenges it (Evans 1989; Nickerson 1998; Kahneman 2011). It is said to operate by selective information searching (e.g. Ask and Granhag 2005; Snyder and Swann 1978; Wason 1968) where information supporting a favoured hypothesis is prioritised over that which does not support it, producing a biased interpretation of the available information (e.g. Snyder and Swann 1978; Wason 1968). Here, information available is interpreted in ways that are partial towards existing beliefs (Ask and Granhag 2005). Seen in an investigative context, the effects of confirmation bias on investigative decision-making is well-documented, with numerous case examples of where it has played a major part in gross miscarriages of justice, such as that of Stefan Kiszko (Roach and Pease 2009) mentioned earlier, or has led to other similarly disastrous investigative failures, such as that of Peter Sutcliffe (aka the Yorkshire Ripper) (e.g. Rossmo 2009; Roach and Pease 2009). Stelfox and Pease (2005) identify confirmation bias to be the common result of adopting an implemental mindset, for example when investigators jump prematurely from the process of 'suspect identification' to 'suspect verification' too early in an investigation process (see Rossmo 2009, for a very good account).

To date, however, extant research into the effects of confirmation bias on investigative decision-making has only focused on how live investigations are/were affected, and not its possible different effects on cold case investigations (including that of homicide). So how might confirmation bias adversely affect investigator decision-making in cold cases? The most obvious answer is in the reviewing of cold cases, which includes not just the review of the initial investigation and evidence, but understanding what is actually meant by the term 'review' in the first place. Rogers' (cited in Marshall 2012) defines the investigative review process as:

> A constructive evaluation of the conduct of an investigation to ensure an objective and thorough investigation has been conducted to national standards which seeks to ensure investigative opportunities are not over-looked and that good practice is identified. (Rogers 2005, p. 3)

That Rogers' definition captures well the necessity for and function of an effective review process in criminal investigation is not disputed here, but what is instead is whether current review processes are set-up exclusively with live investigations in mind and so do not fit well with cold case investigations (Atkin and Roach 2015). The current case review process in England and Wales has several stages (from Fox 2007):

1. Management intervention—review within 24 hours (but within 7 days)—to check that nothing has been missed and confirm staffing.
2. 28-day review or progress review—formal review with a full team utilised
3. Thematic reviews
4. Closure review
5. Peer reviews
6. Cold case reviews
7. Multi-agency reviews (e.g. serious case reviews; MAPPA).
8. Hot de-briefs

Taken as a whole, the current review process looks to be quite thorough, but by the time a case is considered cold, that thoroughness does not appear to be equally applied, with the review of a cold case described thus:

> "If no viable lines of enquiry are left then enter 'investigative maintenance process". (Fox 2007, p. 141)

What that 'maintenance process' actually consists of is unfortunately not elaborated on, with next to no guidance given about the methodology to be adopted in live homicide cases and none given at all about how to prepare for and review cold cases (Atkin and Roach 2015). Although whether reviews of cold cases are actually often proper reviews at all is therefore disputable, whether the frame for cold case review narrow is less so. I suggest that this point is important in cold case investigations for the following reasons:

1. A review of a cold case generally means a review of all the previous reviews and sometimes just the most recent one. If proven to be the case, then any confirmation bias in an initial investigation is likely to remain unrecognised by those 'reviewing' the same case evidence years later.
2. Perhaps more obvious is that a reviewing officer with no new leads to follow is likely to agree with the decision-making of the initial investigator providing the correct procedures have been followed. As was previously suggested, nothing is more likely to excite confirmation bias than the framing of cold cases as 'unsolvable'.
3. As the cold case investigator has to rely on the evidence collected by the initial investigator, they will be in danger of succumbing to a biased interpretation of the information available to them, particularly if the case is a high-profile, famous one then they will have little information with which to refute any hypotheses held by the initial investigator. One can merely speculate here on the objectivity in which investigative decision-making and evidence are recorded by investigators for future investigators to review/use (Atkin and Roach 2015). Research has consistently shown that we are not objective surveyors of our worlds (Rossmo 2009) rather we are influenced by our experiences and expectations (Heuer 1999). Moreover, what we remember depends on what we believe (Begley 2005) and the cold case investigator who remembers a case from the media coverage years before is unlikely to be as objective as the one with no prior knowledge of the case—erroneous or otherwise. I commonly ask students the name of the murdering partner of child killer Ian Huntley. Although most instantly say, Maxine Carr, very few actually remember the important fact that Carr played no part in the killing of the girls, but was sentenced for perverting the cause of justice for giving Huntley a false alibi. When I point this out most remember correctly, but if do not then many would remember her to be a convicted killer.

To recapitulate so far, it is hoped that the reader is now at least a little convinced of the likelihood that cognitive bias can affect investigators of cold case homicides in a number of different ways to those involved with live homicide investigations. Although this hypothesis is based solely on my being a psychologist who has worked with and observed the decision-making of many homicide investigators on both live and cold investigations, the main reason for writing this chapter was to inspire others to conduct empirical research in the area of investigative decision-making in cold cases, or at least to provoke some thinking about it.[4] To this end, this chapter concludes with a brief and tentative agenda for further research.

Cognitive Bias and the Cold Case Investigation: A Tentative Research Agenda

To repeat my central point—cognitive influencers on investigative decision-making are suitably different in form and intensity in live and cold case homicide investigations, to warrant further empirical testing and exploration. They are not the same and so do not require exactly the same thinking and approach. So what is needed? I conclude with a tentative research agenda (presented in no particular order).

First, research focused on the different priming effects that the different types of homicide investigation have on investigators is essential because the words 'live' (current), 'historic' and 'cold case' are more than likely to prime investigators into certain ways of thinking (i.e. framing). As I have maintained to throughout, the term 'cold case' is likely to prime investigators in a different way to the word 'live' case. Reasons are likely to include the fact, and understandably, that cold cases' are less of a priority than the live homicides currently being investigated; the length of time that has passed since the crime means there will be little if nothing new to go on, the lack of new forensic evidence means that an investigative breakthrough is likely; and there is a distinct possibility that the offender has deceased anyway. This list is not exhaustive. These are not likely to be thoughts which cross the mind of the same officer

---

[4] I am currently putting my money where my mouth is and running a series of experiments with police investigators using Decision Board Analysis and I am now lucky enough to have a Ph.D. student currently researching cold case decision-making.

investigating a live homicide. What is needed is research which identifies this framing effect by which a sample of investigators are asked questions relating to their initial thoughts when tasked with 'live', 'historic' and a 'cold case' homicide scenarios. The level and frequency of which System 1 thinking is employed needs to be understood.

Second, research which focuses on variables which affect investigator confidence most in cold case investigations is necessary, and how this is framed is essential if we are to achieve a deeper understanding of how decisions are made and influenced in cold case homicide investigations.

Third, research is needed that focuses on what is actually meant by a 'review' of cold cases, that is what does a review usually entail and what are the common features necessary to trigger a full 'root and branch' review?

Fourth, research to identify whether a difference exists in the way that investigators think about and approach cold cases that are simply undetected and those cold cases that previously led to a miscarriage of justice? One presumes the latter will be more likely to be reviewed in the full sense of the word.

Fifth, cold case reviews are normally conducted by teams and not individuals on their own. Research is needed therefore, which focuses on how group dynamics play a role in inadvertently encouraging cognitive bias, for example one team member's opining that 'there is no point in trying to solve this case', is likely to negatively affect the confidence and conviction of the other team members—particularly where the pessimist is the senior officer.

Sixth (and the last for now) research is needed to show the bias effect of prior knowledge of a case on the cold case investigating officer. As Roach and Pease (2009) suggest, the only way to achieve an objective approach to cold case reviews is to bring in officers with no prior knowledge of it, either from another force or even better, from another country.

This agenda is as tentative as it is exhaustive and should be seen as nothing more than a beginning. I hope that I have (i) warmed-up the thinking and interest around cold case decision-making a little with this chapter, (ii) sown the seeds of an idea with police investigator readers that decision-making in cold-case investigations is not the same as that for live investigation, and (iii) that this needs to be reflected in the guidance and training for police investigators.

REFERENCES

Ask, K., & Granhag, P. A. (2005). Motivational Sources of Confirmation Bias in Criminal Investigations; the Need for Cognitive Closure. *Journal of Investigative Psychology and Offender Profiling, 2,* 43–63.

Ask, K., & Granhag, P. A. (2007). Motivational Bias in Criminal Investigators' Judgments of Witness Reliability. *Journal of Applied Social Psychology, 37*(3), 561–591.

Atkin, H., & Roach, J. (2015). Spot the Difference: Comparing Current and Historic Homicide Investigations in the UK. *Journal of Cold Case Review, 1*(1), 5–21.

Begley, S. (2005). People Believe a 'Fact' That Fits Their Views Even If It's Clearly False. *Science Journal,* p. b1 (Cited in Rossmo, 2009 ibid.).

Borg, M. J., & Parker, K. F. (2001). Mobilizing Law in Urban Areas: The Social Structure of Homicide Clearance Rates. *Law Society Review, 35,* 435–466.

Davis, R. C., Jensen, C. J., Burgette, L., & Burnett, K. (2014). Working Smarter on Cold Cases: Identifying Factors Associated with Successful Cold Case Investigations. *Journal of Forensic Sciences, 59*(2), 375–381. https://doi.org/10.1111/1556-4029.12384.

Dugan, L., Nagin, D. S., & Rosenfield, R. (1999). Explaining the Decline in Intimate Partner Homicide: The Effects of Changing Domesticity, Women's Status, and Domestic Violence Resources. *Homicide Studies, 3*(3), 187–214.

Evans, J. St. B. T. (1989). *Bias in Human Reasoning: Causes and Consequences.* Hillsdale, NJ: Erlbaum.

Fahsing, I., & Ask, K. (2013). Decision Making and Decisional Tipping Points in Homicide Investigations: An Interview Study of British and Norwegian Detectives. *Journal of Investigative Psychology and Offender Profiling, 10,* 155–165.

Fox, J. (2007). Police Investigation in Unexpected Childhood Deaths. In P. Sidebotham & P. Fleming (Eds.), *Unexpected Death in Childhood: A Handbook for Practitioners* (pp. 132–153). Chichester: Wiley.

Gaylor, D. (2002). *Getting Away with Murder: The Re-investigation of Historic Undetected Homicide.* London, UK: Home Office.

Gollwitzer, P. M. (1990). Action Phases and Mindsets. In E. T. Higgins (Ed.), *Handbook of Motivation and Cognition: Foundations of Social Behaviour* (Vol. 2, pp. 53–92). New York: Guidford Press.

Gollwitzer, P. M., Heckhausen, H., & Steller, B. (1990). Deliberative and Implemental Mindsets: Cognitive Tuning Towards Congruous Thoughts and Information. *Journal of Personality and Social Psychology, 59*(6), 119–1127. https://doi.org/10.1037/0022-3514.59.6.1119.

Heur, R. J., Jr. (1999). *Psychology of Intelligence Analysis.* Washington, DC: Center for the Study of Intelligence, Central Intelligence Agency.

Higgins, E. T. (1996). Knowledge Activation: Accessibility, Applicability and Salience. In E. T. Higgins & A. W. Kruglanski (Eds.), *Social Psychology: Handbook of Basic Principles* (pp. 133–168). New York: Guildford Press.

Kahneman, D. (2003). Maps of Bounded Rationality: Psychology for Behavioural Economics. *The American Economic Review, 3*(5), 1449–1475.

Kahneman, D. (2011). *Thinking Fast and Slow.* New York: Farrer, Straus and Giroux.

Marshall, D. (2012). *Effective Investigation of Child Homicide and Suspicious Deaths.* Oxford: Oxford University Press.

McLean, M., & Roach, J. (2011, May). The Trouble with Being Human: Cognitive Bias and the Police Interview. *The Investigator Magazine.*

Nickerson, R. S. (1998). Confirmation Bias: A Ubiquitous Phenomenon in Many Guises. *Review of General Psychology, 2,* 175–220.

Ousey, G. C., & Lee, M. R. (2009). To Know the Unknown: The Decline in Homicide Clearance Rates, 1980–2000. *Criminal Justice Review, 35,* 141–158.

Roach, J. (2012). Long Interval Detections and Under the Radar Offenders. *Journal of Homicide and Major Incident Investigation, 8*(1). Hampshire: ACPO/Centrex.

Roach, J. (2016). No Necrophilia Please, We're British. In L. Mellor, A. Aggrawal, & E. Hickey (Eds.), *Understanding Necrophilia: A Global, Multidisciplinary Approach* (pp. 87–102). San Diego: Cognella.

Roach, J., & Pease, K. (2009). Necropsies and the Cold Case. In D. K. Rossmo (Ed.), *Criminal Investigative Failures* (pp. 327–348). Boca Raton: CRC Press.

Roach, J., & Pease, K. (2014). Police Overestimation of Criminal Career Homogeneity. *Journal of Investigative Psychology and Offender Profiling, 11*(2), 164–178.

Rossmo, D. K. (Ed.). (2009). *Criminal Investigative Failures.* Boca Raton: CRC Press.

Snyder, M., & Swann, W. B. (1978). Hypothesis—Testing Processes in Social Interaction. *Journal of Personality and Social Psychology, 36,* 1202–1212.

Stanovich, K. E., & West, R. F. (2000). Individual Differences in Reasoning: Implications for the Rationality Debate? *Behavioural and Brain Sciences, 23*(5), 645–665.

Stelfox, P. (2008). *Criminal Investigation.* Cullompton: Willan.

Stelfox, P., & Pease, K. (2005). Cognition and Detection: Reluctant Bedfellows? In M. Smith & N. Tilley (Eds.), *Crime Science: New Approaches to Preventing and Detecting Crime.* Cullompton: Willan.

Wason, P. C. (1968). Reasoning About a Rule. *Quarterly Journal of Experimental Psychology, 20,* 273–281.

Wright, M. (2013). Homicide Detectives' Intuition. *Journal of Investigative Psychology and Offender Profiling, 10,* 182–199.

CHAPTER 9

Conclusions

Mark Roycroft

Abstract The authors mentioned certain attributes and skills required
by detectives. Roycroft drew up a "Full decision model" in Chapter 3
and the respective authors have added to this model by helping to define
the decision making process used by effective investigators. We can
now determine the "perfect SIO and decision maker". The perfect SIO
needs good reasoning skills mixed with intuitive and analytical skills. The
authors mentioned the need for good managerial skills and the need to
manage the different phases of an investigation. The characteristics of a
good decision maker are listed at the end of the chapter.

Keywords Management skills · Review · Iterative · Skills · Phasing ·
Reasoning · Heuristics

The preceding chapters have shown the influence of external and internal factors that affect police decision-making in major investigations. The
chapters emphasised the psychological, experiential and skill credentials
required for effective decision-making. The chapters have explored the

M. Roycroft (✉)
Open University, Milton Keynes, UK
e-mail: mark.roycroft@open.ac.uk

© The Author(s) 2019   151
M. Roycroft and J. Roach (eds.),
Decision Making in Police Enquiries and Critical Incidents,
https://doi.org/10.1057/978-1-349-95847-4_9

seven themes that emerged from a historical view of past public inquires and reviews (see Roycroft's Chapter 2). Unfortunately in high pressure, difficult enquires these issues can still occur. These seven issues remain pertinent today when we examine the case of the investigation by Cumbrian police into the death of the infant Poppi Worthington on the 11/12 December 2012 (see Appendix 2). Many of the issues outlined occurred in this case. This further illustrates the need to build on the lessons outlined in this book and for SIOs/decision-makers to consider all the evidence and review that evidence in the way shown here.

All authors mentioned certain attributes and skills required by detectives. Roycroft drew up a "Full decision model" in Chapter 3 and the respective authors have added to this model by helping to define the decision-making process used by effective investigators. Most of the authors mentioned the timing element of good investigations along with the capable phasing of such enquires. Fahsing (Chapter 6) talked of the critical decisions involved along with the tipping points in different enquires. He identified the situational factors and individual factors that influence an investigation. These findings indicate that although expertise seems to make decision-making better, it cannot alone be trusted to serve as a complete safeguard against fundamental cognitive limitations. Enduring high performance in complex operations cannot only rest on individual competence alone. The managerial aspect of effective decision-making was explored by Roycroft and Harland and illustrates the multidimensional aspect to managing an investigative team. Harland's views on the "Major Incident Room" (MIR) management are echoed by Kirby (2013: 113) "where the procedures facilitate checks and balances to reduce human fallibility".

Fahsing's issue of managing the different stages of an enquiry appear to be one of the major "solving factors" in a successful investigation (see Roycroft). Fahsing spoke of the move from suspect identification to verification. Harland in Chapter 5 discussed the timeliness of good investigations along with the sequencing of events. Harland further mentioned the expanding role of the Senior Investigating Officer (SIO) reflecting the extra layers of accountability and governance imposed on SIOs over the last decade.

Investigations in the UK particularly are (correctly) subject to scrutiny by the HMIC, IOPC and Police and Crime Commissioners. They are increasingly subject to internal reviews and public inquires. This places extra emphasis on the need for sound investigative decision making. The acquisition of knowledge (West/Donnelly) and "good coppering" underline how the development of good SIOs and decision-makers is paramount to the success of an investigation. Experience and the attainment of sufficient knowledge to run an investigation are partly achieved through the PIP process and Fahsing describes the benefit of that approach in the UK.

Roycroft explored how the type of case under investigation can influence the outcome of an investigation. Hostile witnesses, lack of forensic opportunities and lack of passive data can all contribute to difficulties in a particular case. All of these can be outside the SIOs control. The SIO can only deal with the "witnesses they are given."

Bringing all the contributions together we can now determine the "perfect SIO and decision maker". Starting with the psychological reasoning skills we can see from all the contributors that the SIO requires an ability to have good reasoning skills mixed with intuitive and analytical skills. While Byrant acknowledges that "it may not always be possible to apply strictly analytical rational models to decision-making" these skills are still vital. The SIO in certain cases will always be subject to "political" pressures from within and without the organisation. This adds another dimension to the perfect SIOs lexicon where they have the managerial qualities needed to "manage" a case over its lifetime and perhaps into review and appeal. West/Donnelly echo the words of Sir Flanagan in the 2004 HMIC report on the Soham case that "grip" of the investigative process is fundamental for success. Success in major investigations in the present day milieu can also mean that the investigation is not subject to judicial, public or media opprobrium. The reputation of individual Forces and the general police service can rise or fall on these type of investigations. The management of these types of enquires also nowadays relies on management of the media and Fahsing describes how "Nowadays, with mass media there is an enormous impact from the first hours—there is absolutely no room for mistakes". As he states, this can have enormous impact on the Norwegian Police Service. In other words it is not only the competence of the enquiry that is at stake it is the perception of competence that can be equally impactive.

The ability to recognise the correct solvability factors and constantly review them over that lifetime are principal skills. The recognition of what solves that particular case and the stages involved in reaching the correct solving factors require skill, experience and management of the "collective brain of the team". Fahsing's suspect identification to verification process requires open-mindedness and reflectiveness almost on an hourly or daily basis. Bryant talks of the ability to apply reasoning skills and a need for self-awareness. Roach along with others mentioned solvability criteria and the influence of cognitive bias mentioned again by several authors. In summary it would appear that the "perfect" SIO is aware of the limitations of cognitive bias and avoiding futile lines of enquiry (see Roycroft replicated actions).

Managing the cycle of information (Harland) and the sequences of events require a form of iterative reasoning. From Fahsing's tipping points, to West/Donnelly's narrative coherence and Roycroft's "stages of investigation"; the phasing and time element of effective decision-making emerge as a key solvability factor.

Roach refers to the unique cycle involved in cold cases and offered a table illustrating the differences (see Chapter 8). He offers the "view" that influencers on investigative decision-making are suitably different in form and intensity in live and cold case homicide investigations and distinguishes between cold case and historic case investigations. This allows for a subtle but distinct difference. Referring again to the Driscoll reinvestigation of the Lawrence case we see this difference well illustrated. The heuristics and reasoning appear to be part experience, part training (PIP) and part innate ability. The ability to avoid bias and provide "sense making" in a rapidly moving milieu are paramount. The good SIO rises above political and situational factors to remain focused on the key points and issues required to solve the case. Roycroft further showed that the decision-making process can differ between different types of investigations. The Soham case and the Milly Dowler case illustrated the need for a twin track approach or a "twin track investigation" s described in Flanagan's report of the Soham case) where there is the likelihood of a simultaneous murder and missing person enquiry.

From DCI Driscoll's (see BBC 2018 Lawrence documentary) "clearing the ground" where returning to review the basics in a cold case illustrates Roach's retrospective Detective "mantra" that good detectives should overcome confirmation bias (Chapter 8), while ignoring political pressures. The need to resist needless activity as shown by the fictitious Captain Renault (mentioned by Harland) and in his case confusing activity with effective investigation illustrate the need to remain focused on the correct lines of enquiry. The assembly of a case over its lifetime requires the correct selection, ordering and emphasis of the investigative material. The rote SIOs identified by Roycroft like Captain Renault confuse activity with effective detective work. While investigations become more complex with the advent of social media, 24/7 news and increased forensic capability the basic ordering and sense making of the material assembled remain at the core of successful investigation. The decision-making required to achieve this aim has been well highlighted by all the authors and a good SIO will require the almost avatar qualities shown to ensure success in an investigation.

In essence the perfect SIO/Decision-maker must:

- Have an ability to review the decision-making process and solvability factors on a regular basis and identify the correct solving factors. This Phasing aspect requires getting "grip" of the investigation in the early stages followed by constant review of the information and decisions, as the case progresses the SIO moves through the decision-making styles i.e.
- Draw on the appropriate legal, forensic and procedural knowledge depending on the enquiry.
- Have an ability to access his/her own experience of a particular theme of enquiry.
- Employing systematic analysis to review evidence. Central to effective decision-making is the idea of diagnostic inclination in which the SIO brings skills and disposition to approach the investigation in a systematic and analytical fashion. The SIO diagnoses an unfamiliar situation and designs a course of action to deal with it. The heuristics that SIOs develop enable them to utilise a framework to understand complex investigations. The SIO needs to be able to identify and apply the appropriate solving factor as well as the simultaneous maintenance of multiple solving factors as critical to the success of an inquiry. The investigation stage shown in Fig. 3.1 (Full decision model in Chapter 3) stressed the importance of the iterations and reframing of the decision-making process.
- Providing clarity of leadership and good management of the team.
- Have an understanding that what the SIO does is important, allowing formulation of alternative hypothesis and not allowing an investigative pathway to be shut down until there is hypothesis confirmation, following systematic reviewing of the assembling evidence.
- There must be a systematic review of the evidence and information which is more effective than simple application of options by rote and

replicating previous practices without appreciating their discriminating power of analysis under different circumstances.

- The SIO must possess the specific skills of knowledge, prioritisation and understand the major incident room procedure.

The above skillset sets a high standard for any SIO to achieve yet this is the reality of any modern investigation.

REFERENCE

Kirby, S. (2013). *Effective Policing*. Palgrave Macmillan.

Appendix 1: Decision Making Book

Code of Ethics

Standards of Professional Behaviour:

1. Honesty and integrity.
2. Authority, respect and courtesy.
3. Equality and diversity I will act with fairness and impartiality.
4. Use of force.
5. Orders and instructions.
6. Duties and responsibilities I will be diligent in the exercise of my duties and responsibilities.
7. Confidentiality I will treat information with respect, and access or disclose it only in the proper course of my duties.
8. Fitness for work I will ensure, when on duty or at work, that I am fit to carry out my responsibilities.
9. Conduct I will behave in a manner, whether on or off duty, which does not bring discredit on the police service or undermine public confidence in policing.
10. Challenging and reporting improper behaviour I will report, challenge or take action against the conduct of colleagues which has fallen below the standards of professional behaviour.

© The Editor(s) (if applicable) and The Author(s), under exclusive licence to Springer Nature Limited 2019
M. Roycroft and J. Roach (eds.), *Decision Making in Police Enquiries and Critical Incidents*,
https://doi.org/10.1057/978-1-349-95847-4

CODE OF ETHICS DECISION MAKING

The Code of Ethics promotes the use of the National Decision Model (NDM) to help embed ethical reasoning in accordance with policing principles and expected standards of behaviour. The model allows people to be more questioning of the situations confronting them, more challenging of themselves and better able to make ethical and effective decisions. The model places the Code of Ethics at the centre of all decision making.

This reminds those in the policing profession that they should consider the principles and expected standards of behaviour set out in the Code at every stage of making decisions. The NDM is inherently flexible. It can be applied to spontaneous incidents or planned operations, by an individual or teams of people, and to operational and non-operational situations. It can also be expanded as appropriate for specialist and other areas of policing. The NDM also works well for reviewing and debriefing decisions and actions.

In every case the elements of the NDM stay the same, but users decide for themselves which questions and considerations they apply at each stage.

Understanding, practising and using the NDM helps people develop the knowledge and skills necessary to make ethical, proportionate and defensible decisions in all policing situations.

In a fast-moving incident, the main priority of decision makers is to keep in mind the principles and standards set out in the Code of Ethics.

What is expected is that you apply the intent of the Code to your decisions and ask yourself questions such as:

- Is my decision in line with the principles and expected behaviours outlined in the Code of Ethics?
- Will this action or decision reflect well on my professionalism and policing generally?
- Would I be comfortable explaining this action or decision to my supervisor?
- Would I be prepared to defend this action or decision in public?

Appendix 2: Management Style

Management style	Exemplar behaviours
Autocratic	SIO makes decisions unassisted by the Major Incident Team (MIT)
	Compartmentalisation of enquiry activities
Democratic	Regular office meetings to ensure adequate intercommunication
	Inclusive decision making
	Detective Inspector I delegated to take charge of specific parts of the enquiry
	"Use the collective brain of the team"
Reactive	Issuing Holmes actions automatically
	Rote behaviours
Proactive	Good use of fast time actions
	Practice use of experts
Innovative	Making brave decisions with an ability to adopt an innovative strategy
	Makes use of novel investigative techniques

© The Editor(s) (if applicable) and The Author(s), 159
under exclusive licence to Springer Nature Limited 2019
M. Roycroft and J. Roach (eds.), *Decision Making
in Police Enquiries and Critical Incidents*,
https://doi.org/10.1057/978-1-349-95847-4

GLOSSARY 2018

ABC: Assume nothing, believe nothing, check everything
Byford report: HMIC report into the Yorkshire Ripper case
Gold Command: Police enquires are sometimes broken down into GoldSilver and Bronze
Holmes: Home Office Large Major Enquiry System

MIR: Major Incident Room
Mirsap: Major Incident Room Standardised Administrative Procedures
PIP: Professionalising Investigative Practice: Detective training in the UK
SOE chart: Sequence of Events chart used in incident rooms
SIO: Senior Investigating Officer; usually a DCI or Det Superintendent
TIE: Trace and, Interview and Eliminate

REFERENCES

ACPO Core Investigative Doctrine. (2005). NPIA (Formerly Centrex). NPCC Murder Manual (Formerly ACPO).

Adhami, E., & Browne, D. (1996). *Major Crime Enquires Improving Expert Support for Detectives*. Police Research Group Special Interest Paper 9.

Ansoff Developed His Classification of Decision-Making in Strategy and Structure. Cambridge: MIT Press, 1962.

Bittner, E. (1967). *The Functions of the Police on Modern Society*. Washington, DC: US Govt.

Bitton, M. (2003). *Wicked Beyond Belief the Hunt for The Yorkshire Ripper*. New York: HarperCollins.

Brookman, F. (2005). *Understanding Homicide*. London: Sage.

Cook, T., & Tattersall, A. (2008). *Blackstone's Senior Investigating Officers' Handbook*. Oxford: Oxford University Press.

CPS Guidance on DNA Charging, Including National Tripartite Protocol, Local FSP Protocol Templates, Staged Reporting Procedure, New MGFSP Form. Harland, 2004.

D'Cruze, S., Walklate, S., & Pegg, S. (2006). *Murder: Social and Historical Approaches to Understanding Murder and Murders*. Portland, OR: Willan.

Donnelly Declan, M. (1999). *The Contribution of the Psychology of Decision Making to Investigative Decision Making in Violent Crime* (MSc thesis). University of Leicester.

Dugan, Nagin, & Rosenfield. (1999). Explaining the Decline in Intimate Partner Homicide: The Effects of Changing Domesticity, Womens Status and Domestic Violence.

© The Editor(s) (if applicable) and The Author(s),
under exclusive licence to Springer Nature Limited 2019
M. Roycroft and J. Roach (eds.), *Decision Making in Police Enquiries and Critical Incidents*,
https://doi.org/10.1057/978-1-349-95847-4

Fahsing and Ask 2013 Roach.

Fiest, A., & Newiss, G. (2004). *Watching the Detectives, Analysing Hard to Solve Homicide Investigations.* London: Home Office.

Fiest a Police Research Group. (1999). *The Effective Use of the Media in Serious Crime Investigations.*

Fisher, H. (1977). *Report into Maxwell Confait Case HMSO.*

Flanagan Report HMIC Review into the Soham Murders.

Home Office Homicide Review 25/04.

Innes, M. (1999). The Media as an Investigative Resource in Murder Enquiries. *British Journal of Criminology, 59*(2, Spring).

Innes, M. (2002a). The Process Structures of Police Homicide Investigations. *British Journal of Criminology, 42*(4), 669–688.

Innes, M. (2002b, March). Symbolic Construction of Murder Investigations. *British Journal of Sociology, 53*(1), 67–87.

Innes, M. (2003). *Investigating Murder Detective Work and the Police Response to Criminal Homicide, Clarendon Studies in Criminology.* Oxford: Oxford University Press.

Innes, M., & Fiest, A. (2004). *Reviewing Murder Investigations an Analysis of Progress Reviews from 6 Police Forces on Line Report 25/04.*

Irving, B., & Dunnighan, C. (1993). *Human Factors in the Quality Control of CID Investigations.* Research No. 201 Criminal Justice.

Kind, S. (1987). *The Scientific Investigation of Crime.* Manchester, UK: Forensic Science Services Limited.

Maguire, N. (1992). *The Conduct and Supervision of Criminal Investigations Research.* Study 5 HMSO.

Maguire, M., Noaks, L., & Hobbs, R. (2003). *Criminal Investigation and Crime Control Handbook of Policing.* London: Willan.

Manning, P. K., & Hawkins, K. (1989). *Police Decision Making.* Presentation for Conference ESRC Police Foundation Gower (pp. 139–156).

Morgan, J. (1979). *Criminal Investigation.* New York: McGraw-Hill.

Morgan, J. (1990). *The Police Function and the Investigation of Crime.* London, UK: Avebury.

Morgan, R., & Newburn, T. (1997). *The Future of Policing.* Oxford: Clarendon Press.

Morrall, P. (2006). *Murder and Society.* Chichester: Wiley.

Mouzos, J., & Muller, D. (2001). *Solvability Factors of Homicide in Australia an Exploratory Analysis October 2001.* www.aic.gov.au.

Nicol, C., Innes, M., Gee, G., & Fiest, A. (2004). *Home Office on Line Report 25/04 Reviewing Murder Investigations, an Analysis of Progress Reviews from Six Police Forces.* London: Home Office.

Reiner, R. (2000). *The Politics of the Police* (3rd ed.). Oxford: Oxford University Press.

Savage, S. (2000). *Core Issues in Policing* (2nd ed.). Harlow: Longman.

Smith, N., & Flanagan, C. (2000). *The Effective Detective: Identifying the Skills of an Effective SIO*. London: Police Research Group, Home Office.

Stelfox, P. (2008). *Dictionary of Policing* (Newburn and Neyroud Willan, Eds.).

The Damilola Taylor Review. (2002, December).

The Journal of Homicide and Major Incident Investigation. (2008). Historical Analysis of Public Inquiries of Homicide Investigations, 4(2, Autumn), 43–58.

The Shipman Inquiry. (2003). *2nd Report the Police Investigation of 1998*. Chairman Dame Janet Smith OBE HMSO.

Wellford, C., & Cronin, J. (2000). *An Analysis of Variables Affecting the Clearance of Homicide: A Multivariate Study* (43 Pages Research). Washington, DC: Justice Research and Statistics Association. www.jrsa.org.

West, A. (2000, August). Clinical Assessment of Homicide Offenders. *Homicide Studies, 4*(3), 219–233.

West, A. (2001). From Offender Profiler to Behavioural Investigative Advisor. *Police Research and Management, 5*(1), 95–108.

Website

Authorised Professional Practice and can be found at https://www.app.college.police.uk/app-content/major-investigation-and-public-protection/homicide/.

INDEX